Understanding Gender in Maldives

DIRECTIONS IN DEVELOPMENT
Countries and Regions

Understanding Gender in Maldives

Toward Inclusive Development

Jana El-Horr and Rohini Prabha Pande

WORLD BANK GROUP

Contents

Preface   ix
About the Contributors   xi
Executive Summary   xiii
Abbreviations   xv

Chapter 1   **Introduction**   1
             Background and Justification   1
             Organizing Framework   2
             Data and Methods   5
             Report Road Map   6
             Notes   6
             References   7

Chapter 2   **The Context for Gender Differentials in Maldives**   9
             Introduction   9
             Formal Institutions   9
             Maldives' Economic Development   14
             Informal Institutions: Politics, Society, Culture,
                 and Religion   15
             Notes   18
             References   19

Chapter 3   **Gender Differentials in Outcomes**   23
             Introduction   23
             Gender Differentials in the Private Sphere: Agency   23
             Gender Differentials in the Public Sphere: Agency   27
             Gender Differentials in the Public Sphere: Education
                 and Health Endowments   29
             Gender Differentials in the Public Sphere: Employment
                 and Income Opportunities   34
             Decline in Support for Gender Equality   42
             Notes   46
             References   47

Chapter 4   Conclusion and Recommendations   **51**
             Summary and Conclusions   51
             Recommendations   53
             A Final Word on Approaches for Programming   60
             References   61

Boxes

1.1   Key Definitions   3
2.1   Changing Culture and Society in Maldives in the 21st Century   16
3.1   Reproductive Health in Maldives: Lacking for Both Men
       and Women   33
3.2   Gangs and Unemployment among Young Maldivian Men   41

Figures

1.1   WDR 2012 Framework: Societal Determinants of
       Gender Outcomes   3
1.2   Modified WDR 2012 Framework   4
2.1   Modified World Development Report Framework—Focus
       on Context   10
2.2   Contextual Factors Supporting or Hindering Gender Equality   10
2.3   Corruption Ranking, Maldives and Other Selected Countries   11
2.4   Dynamics of Youth Disconnect in Maldives   18
3.1   World Development Report Modified Framework—Focus
       on Outcomes   24
3.2   Women's Reports of Decision Making in the Household   24
3.3   Gender Differentials in Ownership of Assets and Resources   25
3.4   Reported Lifetime Partner/Nonpartner Physical or
       Sexual Violence   27
3.5   Gender Differentials in Educational Enrollment in Maldives   30
3.6   Gender Differentials in Current Activity among Youth,
       by Residence   31
3.7   Achievement in Higher Education, by Sex   31
B3.1.1 Women Reporting Having Ever Used Modern Contraception   33
3.8   Age- and Sex-Specific Rate of Economic Activity   35
3.9   Unemployment Rate by Age and Gender   36
3.10   Women's Reported Reasons for Unemployment   37
3.11   Men's Reported Reasons for Unemployment   37
3.12   Percent of Employees Who Are Women, by Industry   38
3.13   Youth Unemployment by Age, Sex, and Location   40
3.14   Agreement with Statement "A Man Should Never Hit His Wife"   43
3.15   Change in Support for Women's Right to Refuse Marital Sex   44
3.16   Change in Support for Gender Equality: Rural Areas   44
3.17   Change in Support for Gender Equality: Urban Areas   45
3.18   Women's Representation in the People's Majlis   45

3.19   Support for Women's Rights in Maldives Tilting Away from
        Gender Equality   46
4.1   Key Aspects of Female Disadvantage in Maldives   52
4.2   Key Aspects of Male Disadvantage in Maldives   52

Tables
3.1   Changes in Gender Differences in Attitudes toward Gender
        Equality, by Sex of Respondent and Year   42
4.1   Summary of Recommendations   55

Preface

The study was led by Jana El-Horr (Social Development Specialist, GSURR) under the guidance of Maria Correia (Lead Social Development, GSURR), Jennifer Solotaroff (Senior Social Development Specialist, GSURR), and David Warren (Practice Manager, GSURR). The core team comprised Rohini Prabha Pande (Senior Gender Consultant), Sandra Ruckstuhl (Social Development Consultant), Tanya D'Lima (Consultant, GSURR), and Dustin Smith (Consultant, GSURR).

The team greatly appreciates guidance provided by Somil Nagpal (Senior Health Specialist, GHNDR), Harsha Aturupane (Lead Education Specialist, GEDDR), Silvia Redaelli (Senior Economist, GPVDR), Mari Shojo (Education Specialist, GEDDR), and feedback and advice from the Maldives Country Management Unit. The team thanks Aminath Inasha Shafeeq for her support through the country missions and collection of qualitative data.

In preparing the study, the team benefited greatly from detailed comments received from peer reviewers Wendy Cunningham (Program Leader, LCC1C), Helene Rex (Senior Social Development Specialist, GSURR), Shubha Chakravarty (Economist, GCGDR), Ioana Botea (Consultant, AFRGI), Alys Willman (Senior Social Development Specialist, GSURR), Helle Buchhave (Gender Specialist, GSURR), Rifat Hassan (Health Specialist, GHNDR), Changqing Sun (Senior Economist, GSPDR), Matthew Morton (Social Protection Specialist, GSPDR), and Shalika Subasinghe (Consultant, GSPDR).

Finally, the team expresses gratitude to all the stakeholders who shared their expertise and all the women and men in Maldives who were interviewed for this report.

About the Contributors

TANYA D'LIMA is a social development consultant who has worked for the World Bank on several research initiatives and projects related to youth inclusion and gender-based violence. Tanya has also consulted with UN Women (United Nations Entity for Gender Equality and the Empowerment of Women) on the promotion of gender-inclusive cities. Prior to this, she worked for the Asia division of Search for Common Ground—an international conflict resolution organization based in Washington, DC. She has an MA in international development and social change from Clark University.

JANA EL-HORR is a Social Development Specialist at the World Bank in the South Asia Region. Prior to joining the World Bank, Ms. El-Horr worked extensively in Iraq and Lebanon on postconflict reconstruction and economic inclusion of women and youth. Ms. El-Horr holds a doctorate in conflict studies from George Mason University, and a BA in economics from the American University of Beirut.

ROHINI PRABHA PANDE is a Senior Gender Consultant at the World Bank. Prior to this, Dr. Pande worked at the International Center for Research on Women (ICRW), leading intervention research programs in South Asia that focused on adolescent reproductive health and empowerment. She has also worked with the Rockefeller and Ford Foundations, Care International, and other nongovernmental organizations (NGOs) in South Asia and West Africa on female education, women's income generation, and women's empowerment. She has a ScD from the Johns Hopkins Bloomberg School of Public Health and an MPA from Princeton University's Woodrow Wilson School of Public and International Affairs.

SANDRA M. RUCKSTUHL is a social development and governance specialist who provides applied research services, capacity building, and advisory support to sustainable development policy and operations in countries worldwide. Dr. Ruckstuhl has worked with the World Bank, United Nations, and U.S. government in more than 20 countries, conducting analysis, writing operational guidance, and providing training to promote collaborative governance, social inclusion, and equitable benefits from investments. Dr. Ruckstuhl earned her BA in international studies at University of Wisconsin-Madison and completed her MSc and PhD at George Mason University's School for Conflict Analysis and Resolution.

DUSTIN ANDREW SMITH is a gender consultant with the World Bank South Asia Region's Social Development Unit. His research interests include the sociocultural norms underlying gender inequality in South Asia as well as the relationship between women and law in the region. He has a master of divinity from Harvard University, where his culminating thesis sought to assess and to envision an appropriate response to the phenomenon of forced marriage among South Asian communities in the United States. In addition, Mr. Smith has a BS from Brandeis University in Waltham, Massachusetts.

Executive Summary

Within the past decade Maldives has moved from low- to middle-income status, introduced democracy, and been hailed as a Millennium Development Goal Plus country. Unlike in much of South Asia, women face little discrimination in basic aspects of life such as education, health, and survival; however, gender inequality exists. Specifically, Maldives exhibits a classic case of a relatively prosperous country where gender inequalities in basic well-being are largely diminished but where other social and cultural gendered restrictions, especially on women's roles within and outside the home, persist and may be expanding.

An insufficiently inclusive model of economic development forms the backdrop for gender dynamics in Maldives. Additionally, despite several gender-egalitarian laws, persistent deficiencies in law and governance hamper improvements in gender equality. Improvements are also hampered by a conservative shift in family structure and religious life toward rigid, inegalitarian roles for men and women. Finally, youth are growing increasingly disconnected from family and society and traditional identities that defined their transition to adulthood, a situation that poses particular risks for young men.

Gender differentials are nuanced in work and schooling. Women's labor force participation is high but limited to lower echelons of the economy. Women are slightly more likely than men to be unemployed. There is no gender bias in primary and secondary schooling, but girls' access to tertiary and professional education is curbed by beliefs about girls' and women's mobility and primacy of household roles over others. Within the home, women face challenges that men do not, such as high risks of domestic violence and little control over household assets. Finally, women have limited presence in local and national politics and governance.

Men face different gendered consequences. Shifts in notions of masculinity from gender egalitarian to increasingly conservative preferences for the separation of gender roles inside and outside the home place the onus of earning on young men. At the same time, young men are dissatisfied with current economic options, and youth unemployment is high. This disaffection, combined with a lack of strong alternative social structures to replace the breakdown of traditional family structures that has accompanied Maldives' development trajectory, appear to be propelling young men toward greater social conservatism, participation in gangs, drug use, and violence.

Overall, women are more disadvantaged in more realms of life than are men. Moreover, public support for gender equality and women's rights on various aspects of life appears to be declining, particularly as regards work and family interactions. These developments are worrying for the future of gender equality in Maldives, as well as for a more inclusive development model that would offer opportunities to both men and women, in youth and adulthood.

Abbreviations

ADB	Asian Development Bank
CAS	country assistance strategy
CEDAW	Convention to Eliminate All Forms of Discrimination Against Women
CGAP	country gender action plan
CMU	country management unit
DGFPS	Department of Gender and Family Protection Services
DHS	Demographic and Health Surveys
EFA	Education for All
EU	European Union
FGD	focus group discussion
GBV	gender-based violence
GDP	gross domestic product
GoM	Government of Maldives
HIES	Household Income and Expenditure Survey
HRC	Human Rights Commission
IDA	International Development Association
IFES	International Foundation for Electoral Systems
ILO	International Labour Organization
LSMS	Living Standards Measurement Study
MDG	Millennium Development Goal
MPAO	Maldives Pension Administration Office
MSMEs	micro, small, and medium enterprises
MVR	Maldivian rufiyaa
NEA	not economically active
NEET	not in employment, education, or training
NGO	nongovernmental organization
PAD	project appraisal document (of the World Bank)
SCD	Systematic Country Diagnostic (of the World Bank)
TVET	technical and vocational education and training
UN	United Nations
UNDAF	United Nations Development Assistance Framework
UNDP	United Nations Development Programme
UNFPA	United Nations Population Fund

UNICEF	United Nations Children's Fund
UN Women	United Nations Entity for Gender Equality and the Empowerment of Women
USAID	United States Agency for International Development
WDC	women's development committee
WDR	World Development Report
WHO	World Health Organization

CHAPTER 1

Introduction

Background and Justification

Maldives stands at a crossroads where economic fissures, political tensions, and social fragmentation juxtaposed with efforts to establish democratic practice could have a significant influence on gender equality and, indeed, development outcomes more broadly. The devastation of the 2004 tsunami opened the country to international donors, which facilitated a period of rapid growth and Maldives' advancement to middle-income status. The period of rapid growth also helped the country to make significant progress in meeting five of the eight Millennium Development Goals (MDGs) and to be recognized as an MDG Plus country in South Asia. At the same time, although ahead of other South Asian countries on many aspects of gender equality, Maldives has not attained MDG 3—the goal for gender equality and women's empowerment (Department of National Planning 2010).

The reality of gender equality in Maldives is dichotomous: in the public realm, gender equality (including situations where women fare better than men) exists in education, health, survival, and labor force participation, where fairly liberal and egalitarian laws, policies, and institutions appear to enable relative gender equality. In contrast, in the private sphere where social conservatism is more dominant and consequently Sharia law is more likely to be followed, there is a steady but less researched shift toward gender inequality in gender relations, power, and roles within the household and in intimate relationships, such as in marriage (including divorce and intimate partner violence) and in the division of decision making and assets between partners or spouses. Research conducted for this report and other secondary literature argue that increasing social conservatism and this dichotomy between gender differentials in the private and public spheres of life could slow, and even reverse, Maldives' gains in gender equality in education, health, and other developmental outcomes.

The future of gender equality is thus an immediate developmental concern for Maldives. However, this phenomenon is often overlooked for three reasons. First, in the South Asia region Maldives is viewed as a relative success because gender inequalities in visible indicators such as survival, health, education, employment, and mobility are significantly lower than in neighboring countries. Second, the well-documented gender-egalitarian nature of Maldivian civil laws often over-shadows the small amount of social research that documents the patriarchal nature of Maldivian households and Sharia law. Finally, social and cultural norms in Maldives have, until recently, been relatively moderate and only in the last decade have started to veer toward a more patriarchal view of gender relations. As this report will illustrate, this shift away from gender-egalitarian norms is detrimental to gender equality across various spheres of Maldivian life, mostly for women but also in some cases for men. The following four specific questions are addressed in this report:

1. *What are the institutional underpinnings of gender equality (or the lack thereof) in Maldives?*
   How do the laws and constitution of the land provide for gender equality? How do gender differentials manifest in political participation at national and local levels?
2. *How do gender differentials manifest in relations between men and women in the private sphere of the household?*
   What are the key gender differentials in the sphere of the household, for out-comes such as decision making, control over household assets, and exposure to domestic violence? What role does the institutional and cultural environment play in perpetuating gender differentials in intimate relations?
3. *How do gender differentials manifest in the interaction between men and women in the public sphere of society, economy, and politics?*
   How do gender differentials manifest in the public sphere, in outcomes like education, health, employment, vulnerability to violence outside the home, and political participation? How does the institutional and cultural environ-ment influence these gender differentials?
4. *What do recent trends say about the future of gender relations in Maldives?*
   What are the trends in gender differentials in Maldives across a range of economic and social outcomes? In particular, how is Maldives' particular juxtaposition of increasingly conservative social and cultural norms, on the one hand, and officially gender-egalitarian formal institutions, on the other hand, influencing improvements or reversals in gender equality?

Organizing Framework

A modified version of the framework conceptualizing the links between gender equality and development in the 2012 *World Development Report* (WDR 2012) on Gender Equality and Development (World Bank 2011) provides the organiz-ing framework for this report. Box 1.1 provides the definitions we use for key concepts within this framework.

The WDR 2012 framework (figure 1.1) posits that formal institutions (those related to law and governance), markets, and informal institutions (those related to social norms and beliefs) interact to influence household decision making.

Box 1.1 Key Definitions

Gender refers to the social, behavioral, and cultural attributes, expectations, and norms associated with being a woman or a man.

Gender differentials: We use the term "gender differentials" as equivalent to the concept of "gender equality" to clarify that the focus is on different and (un)equal distribution of economic, social, or political resources between men and women.

Formal institutions include the national constitution and civil law, Sharia law, and government policies relevant to gender equality.

Informal institutions refer to the state of, trends in, and interaction between Maldives' political system, social norms, cultural shifts, and changes in religious practices and beliefs.

Markets are interpreted for the purposes of this report as representing the particular economic development experience of Maldives.

The *"private" sphere* is defined as relationships between intimates and within the family. Therefore, in this analysis, outcomes measuring gender differentials in the private sphere include those aspects of agency that influence intimate relationships, namely, household decision making, control over household assets and resources, and vulnerability to violence.

The *"public" sphere* is characterized by interactions in the broader social, political, and market environments. Therefore, in this analysis, outcomes measuring gender differentials in the public sphere include those aspects of agency that concern gender equality in public mobility and political participation, endowments such as health and education, and economic opportunities reflected in labor force participation, wages, and income.

Figure 1.1 WDR 2012 Framework: Societal Determinants of Gender Outcomes

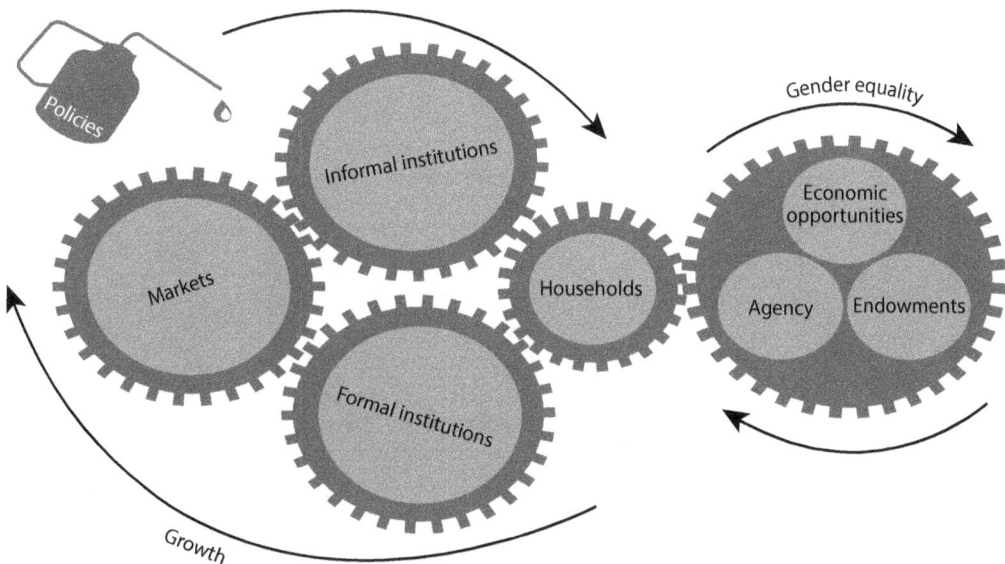

Source: World Bank 2011.
Note: Gender outcomes result from interactions among households, markets, and institutions.

Subsequent household choices determine the nature, direction, and extent of gender differentials in economic, social, and political outcomes. The framework conceptualizes gender equality in development outcomes as defined by the inter-action of three components: (1) agency (defined as the ability to make choices and informed decisions on all aspects of life, including economic, political and familial relations, and personal safety), (2) endowments (that is, investments such as education and health status), and (3) opportunities (such as labor force par-ticipation). The use of "gears" illustrates the interconnectedness of gender equal-ity with households and society as a whole. Thus, what happens in any one realm or gear influences the whole system toward either greater gender equality and greater development or worse gender equality and stalling development.

The Public and Private Spheres

The concepts of "public" and "private" spheres of life have been used in the social sciences for some time (Gavison 1992; Weintraub 1997). We use these concepts here to modify the WDR framework in two ways (figure 1.2). First, we further unpack the components of gender equality (agency, endowments, and opportunities) into those that relate to outcomes in the public spheres of life and those that relate to outcomes in the private spheres of life.[1] In particu-lar, we disentangle the concept of agency into "agency—private realm" (for intrahousehold relations) and "agency—public realm" (for interactions with community and society outside of the household). Thus, the right-most gear in figure 1.2 now includes four components. Second, we posit that each of these four components of gender equality is a gear in itself, such that change in one

Figure 1.2 Modified WDR 2012 Framework

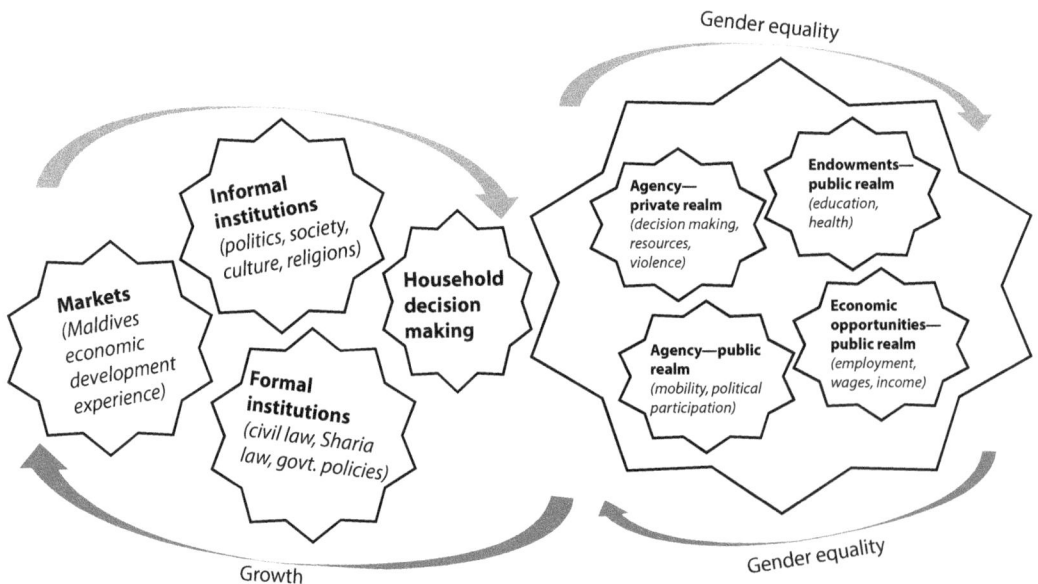

component of gender equality will influence other components of gender equality. Further, gender differentials in the public and private spheres do not always move in the same direction. Finally, as in the original framework, economic growth and the formal institutions of civil law and policy are conceptualized to interact with the informal institutions of politics and religious and social norms to influence how households make decisions regarding gender equality in the public and private spheres.

Data and Methods

This report draws primarily on a range of secondary sources of data, with some triangulation via primary data collected through key informant interviews and focus group discussions (FGDs).

Main sources of secondary qualitative and quantitative data include the following:

- *Maldivian government data and documents*: Government statistical yearbooks on education, compilations of data on the country's health profile, and data and analyses from the 2006 and 2014 census.
- *Information and reports from nonprofits*: Reports by Maldives Human Rights Commission, International Foundation for Electoral Systems (IFES), and Maldivian nongovernmental organizations (NGOs) such as Hope for Women.
- *Reports from multilateral organizations and other donors*: Reports by the Asian Development Bank (ADB), the International Labour Organization (ILO), the United Nations Development Programme (UNDP), the United Nations Population Fund (UNFPA), the United Nations Children's Fund (UNICEF), and the World Health Organization (WHO).
- *World Bank reports* on Maldives.
- *Survey data*: These include—but are not limited to—data on household structure, youth, reproductive health, other health indicators, and women's empowerment from the 2009 Maldives Demographic and Health Survey; global comparators for education, health, and other indicators from the World Development Indicators; and data on income and employment from the Household Income and Expenditure Survey (HIES) and statistics provided by the ILO.

The team also analyzed peer-reviewed publications recommended by Maldivian scholars. This academic literature covered qualitative and quantitative research on Maldives, on other South Asian countries, and on countries that are considered by those familiar with Maldives to be appropriate comparisons, such as Indonesia and Malaysia. Sources included journal articles, books, and doctoral theses.

Key informant interviews and focus group discussions were conducted in Washington, DC, and in Maldives (on Malé and Dharavandhoo Islands) between January and February 2015. The study team interviewed different ministries in Maldives and 33 individuals from 16 organizations in Washington, DC, and Malé, including the World Bank. Two FGDs were held on Dharavandhoo Island. One was convened with a subsample of the island's population, a convenience sample comprising about 50 individuals who attended a presentation on a recent World Bank report on the situation of youth in Maldives (World Bank 2014). The second discussion convened a purposively selected sample of owners and staff of the island's tourist guesthouses. Key informant interviews and focus group discussions were conducted based on interview guides with open-ended questions designed to prompt a conversation on gender, youth, and related issues and policies. The discussions were not audiotaped, and thus direct quotes cannot be provided. However, detailed notes were taken and have been used as transcripts for analysis. Each transcript was assigned a unique identification number so that data from each interview could be shared without compromising individual confidentiality. Transcripts were analyzed using codes to capture information on indicators derived from the WDR 2012 framework adapted for this report. Each transcript was entered into an Excel document and was coded accordingly.[2] This process enabled the team to systematically sort and analyze information from the interviews on each theme of interest.

Report Road Map

Chapter 2 describes the context of gender differentials—specifically, the patterns in formal and informal institutions and markets as they influence gender dynamics in Maldives. This chapter provides an overview of three areas: policy and law, economic development, and politics, society, culture, and religion.

Chapter 3 analyzes gender differentials in the private and public realms as presented in figure 1.2, using the most recent qualitative and quantitative data available. Analysis highlights, where possible, regional differences between Malé and the atolls, and trends over time. Given that half the country consists of youth under the age of 25, we elaborate on patterns of gender differentials specific to youth where data allow such a focus.

Chapter 4 provides a summary of conclusions and a list of recommendations to address gender differentials.

Notes

1. There are multiple ways to define the public and private spheres, and definitions can change according to context. For this report, the public/private distinction differentiates between the "private" world of relationships between intimates and within the family and the "public" world of interactions in broader social, political, or market environments, or between domestic and nondomestic life (Gavison 1992; Weintraub 1997).

2. Excel can be used for qualitative data analysis in the absence of dedicated qualitative analysis statistical tools (Meyer and Avery 2009).

References

Department of National Planning, Republic of Maldives. 2010. *Millennium Development Goals: Maldives Country Report 2010*. Malé, Maldives: Government of Maldives.

Gavison, R. 1992. "Feminism and the Public/Private Distinction." *Stanford Law Review* 41 (1): 1–45.

Meyer, Daniel Z., and Leanne M. Avery. 2009. "Excel as a Qualitative Data Analysis Tool." *Field Methods* 21 (1): 91–112.

Weintraub, J. 1997. "The Theory and Politics of the Public/Private Distinction." In *Public and Private in Thought and Practice: Perspectives on a Grand Dichotomy*, edited by Jeff Weintraub and Krishan Kumar, 1–42. Chicago: University of Chicago Press.

World Bank. 2011. *World Development Report 2012. Gender Equality and Development*. Washington, DC: World Bank.

———. 2014. *Youth in Maldives: Shaping a New Future for Young Women and Men through Engagement and Empowerment*. Washington, DC: World Bank.

CHAPTER 2

The Context for Gender Differentials in Maldives

Introduction

We start with an overview of the context within which households make decisions and gender relations play out in Maldives, specifically, the formal institutions of governance, laws, and policy; the market forces of the country's experience of economic development; and the informal institutions of society, culture, and religion (figure 2.1).

There are a number of contextual factors in the Maldives that are supportive of gender equality (figure 2.2). Primary among these, our analysis shows, are guarantees of gender equality in the Maldivian constitution, rapid economic growth, and the achievement of multiple Millennium Development Goals (MDGs) that create a society with multiple opportunities, few traditional restrictions on women (unlike much of South Asia), and a traditionally liberal version of Islam. Yet other contextual conditions work to dampen the salutary effect of factors supportive of gender equality. Key among these are a limited capacity in the government to implement gender-equitable laws and policies, a broadly non-inclusive economic development model, increasing conservatism, and a rising disconnect among youth with the society they inhabit. The rest of this chapter elaborates on these dynamics.

Formal Institutions

Political Instability, Lack of Good Governance, and Corruption

Maldives has gone through rapid political transformation in the last decade. The first democratic elections in Maldives were held in 2008. However, democracy continues to be fragile and institutions are weak. The first-ever elected president resigned in 2012, and escalating political tension has dominated Maldivian public life since. In the midst of this instability, accountability is low and corruption remains high.[1] Transparency International's Corruption Perception Index ranked Maldives 134th of 182 countries in 2011; this represents a drop of 57 places

Figure 2.1 Modified World Development Report Framework—Focus on Context

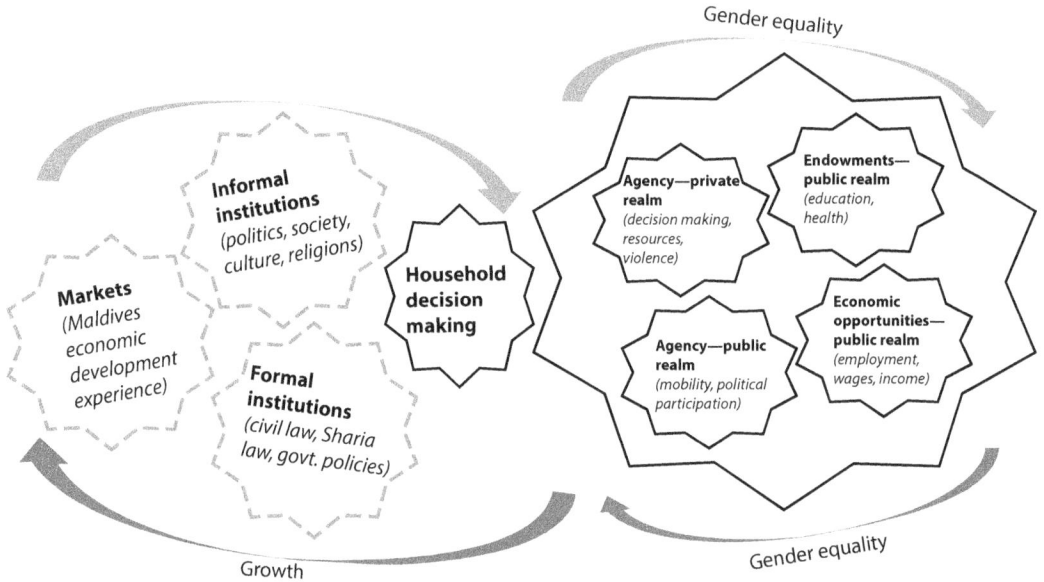

Gender equality

Informal institutions
(politics, society, culture, religions)

Markets
(Maldives economic development experience)

Formal institutions
(civil law, Sharia law, govt. policies)

Household decision making

Agency—private realm
(decision making, resources, violence)

Endowments—public realm
(education, health)

Agency—public realm
(mobility, political participation)

Economic opportunities—public realm
(employment, wages, income)

Growth

Gender equality

Figure 2.2 Contextual Factors Supporting or Hindering Gender Equality

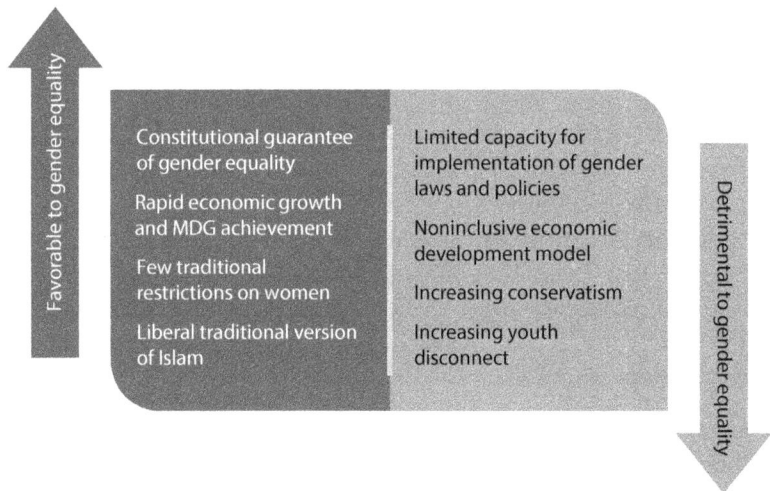

Favorable to gender equality

Constitutional guarantee of gender equality

Rapid economic growth and MDG achievement

Few traditional restrictions on women

Liberal traditional version of Islam

Limited capacity for implementation of gender laws and policies

Noninclusive economic development model

Increasing conservatism

Increasing youth disconnect

Detrimental to gender equality

since the country first appeared in this index in 2008. As shown in figure 2.3, only two other South Asian countries, Afghanistan and Nepal, fare worse with regard to corruption, and Maldives has a worse ranking than socially comparable countries such as Malaysia, Indonesia, or Mauritius[2] (Transparency International 2011). Furthermore, in Transparency International's Maldives' Global Corruption Barometer Survey in 2013, a large majority of respondents perceived that

Figure 2.3 Corruption Ranking, Maldives and Other Selected Countries

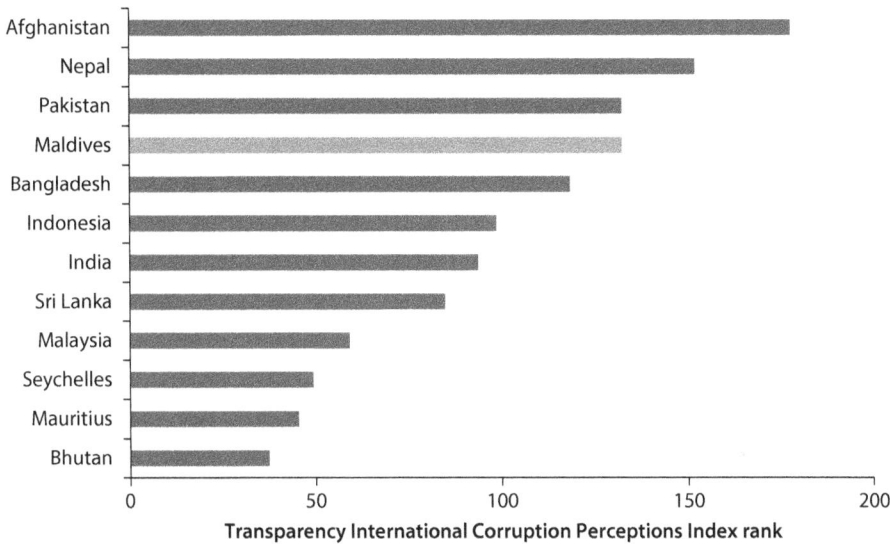

Source: Transparency International 2011.

corruption had gotten worse over the preceding two years (83 percent), that the government was corrupt (97 percent), and that the country was governed by a minority that acted in its own interests (96 percent) (Transparency International 2013). News and commentary in local and international media describe corruption as pervasive in the Maldivian judiciary, security apparatus, and political decision making.[3] Key informant interviews corroborate this secondary source evidence.

Constitutional and Legal Guarantees of Gender Equality

The country's constitution guarantees equal access for women and men to the rights and freedoms provided by it, and the government is tasked with ensuring constitutional equality (UN Women and UNDP 2014). Maldives is also a signatory to a range of international laws and regulations on gender equality (albeit with reservations in the adoption of international conventions where they are deemed to violate Sharia law), including the Convention to Eliminate All Forms of Discrimination Against Women (CEDAW), the Beijing Platform for Action for women's rights, and the Cairo Plan of Action for reproductive and sexual rights. In 2009, a National Gender Equality Policy was established. It instructs all agencies of government "… to address women's issues … recognizing that women and men have different needs and priorities" (ADB 2014). Most policies in the public spheres of health, education, employment, and political participation specifically outlaw discrimination on the basis of sex.

In 1997 the Constitution of Maldives was amended to declare Maldives an Islamic state. Consequently, the legal system has been characterized by a combination of civil and Sharia law. For instance, Islamic (Sharia) law covers areas of family, evidence, and criminal laws, whereas civil law covers other areas. Most broadly, judges are constitutionally required to refer to the Constitution and to laws passed by the Majlis, the Maldivian parliament. In cases where either of these sources is silent, Sharia rules hold (Al Suood 2014).

Gendered Aspects of Employment, Education, and Health-Related Civil Laws and Policies

Laws in Maldives are relatively gender equitable on matters in the public sphere such as employment, education, and health. The 2008 Employment Act, the most recent law on employment, outlines provisions for equal access to employment for men and women, prohibits the use of sex or marital status as grounds for dismissal from any job, and includes generous provisions for maternity leave. Notably the act also prohibits employers from using familial responsibility as a cause to dismiss an employee (Ministry of Human Resources, Youth and Sport, n.d.). Given that women are more likely than men to be juggling professional and familial responsibility, this provision is especially important for legal equality of employment opportunity for men and women. Other laws provide for women's participation in cooperatives and women's representation on corporate boards (ADB 2014).

The government's Education Master Plan 2007–2011/2016 and its Education for All (EFA) mid-decade assessment highlight gender parity and quality of education as key cross-cutting issues important to improve education in Maldives (ADB 2014). Health policy documents recognize health as a human right and mandate health care for all citizens. The strategic framework for the government's National Reproductive Health Strategy for 2014–18 includes gender equality as a key underlying value and principle (Government of Maldives, n.d.; Ministry of Health and Gender 2014; WHO 2013).

Civil Laws for Women's Political Participation

In both public and private spheres, efforts are ongoing to tackle barriers to women's political participation. In 2008 the constitutional ban on women standing for president was removed. Although there are no quotas for women in local or national governments, multiple initiatives and policies attempt to increase women's political participation. For instance, the Ministry of Law and Gender is tasked with increasing women's participation not just in politics but also in economic, social, and cultural realms—this task was previously housed at the Department of Gender and Family Protection Services (DGFPS) (UNDP 2011). In another example, the Decentralization Act of 2010 mandates that local councils have Island Women Development Committees as an integral part of local governance (Hope for Women 2012).

Sharia Law in the Private Sphere

Whereas civil law typically holds primacy for matters that fall in the public sphere, Sharia law has primacy for matters that fall in the private sphere. This dichotomy can undermine some gender-egalitarian aims of civil laws and policies. For instance, family law (where Sharia law is often applied) permits polygamy and prohibits marriage between Maldivian women and non-Muslim men (though not the other way around). Also, women's evidence is not considered equivalent to men's evidence in matters such as extramarital sex or rape, putting women at a disadvantage in cases that involve abuse (ADB 2007). It should be noted that such discriminatory provisions do not necessarily reflect any inherent gender bias in Islam per se; rather, "… current cultural views on the superiority of men over women have overshadowed the progressiveness of Islam, resulting in interpretations that tend to discriminate against women in areas such as marriage and property rights, access to employment and livelihoods, and participation in decision making in the home and community" (ADB 2014).

Government Attempts to Legislate Gender Equality in the Private Sphere

Recent governmental legislative, policy, and programmatic initiatives have attempted to overcome gender inequality in the private sphere and counter some of the discriminatory practices reflected in Sharia law. The Family Law Act (2001) was the first law specifically related to gender relations. This act set a minimum age at marriage and annulled men's right to divorce their wives by reciting a verbal formula (ADB 2007). The Draft National Gender Policy has recognized traditional, customary, and cultural practices that harm women and girls as a violation of human rights (UNDP 2011). In the first half of the 2000s, the Ministry of Arts, Environment and Culture and other government bodies worked with media on awareness campaigns to promote gender inclusion and highlight positive images of women and their roles (Institute of Social Studies Trust 2008). The Domestic Violence Prevention Act, which came into effect in April 2012, prohibits domestic violence and establishes clear guidelines for prevention, support to survivors, prosecution of perpetrators, and the role of different state authorities in implementing these provisions (Shareef, n.d.).

The country's legal record for women's protection, however, remains mixed. Although the Government of Maldives has passed a number of laws designed to address gender-based violence in recent years, including the Sexual Harassment and Prevention Act (2014), laws pertaining to marital rape continue to be absent (Solotaroff and Pande 2014). Maldives does not implement all aspects of Sharia law relating to perceived sexual "crimes," but certain practices, such as flogging, are applied. Controversial provisions that criminalize extramarital sexual relations, or *zina*, persist, and men are rarely convicted (Solotaroff and Pande 2014). Those convicted of *zina* crimes are often subject to public lashings. In almost all cases, the victims of this practice are women.[4] Rape is interpreted as "forced *zina*," and the presence of four male witnesses or a confession are the only valid forms of evidence, thus making it unlikely for a female victim to obtain justice, or even to attempt restitution (Solotaroff and Pande 2014). The increasing influence of conservative, patriarchal social norms in Maldives makes these lacunae even more worrisome.

Understanding Gender in Maldives · http://dx.doi.org/10.1596/978-1-4648-0868-5

Organizational Instability within Government Structures to
Address Gender Issues

These dynamics are occurring against the backdrop of several decades of instability within the governmental structures to address gender concerns. The government structures tasked with policy mandates to address gender issues have
shifted multiple times over the last 25 years. A Gender Committee formed in
1979 was declared a Gender Department in 1989, and then in 1993 it grew to
be the Gender Ministry. However, since then, the name of the Gender Ministry,
where it sits in the larger structure of the government, its mandate, and its work
portfolios have continued to shift (Department of National Planning 2012;
Hope for Women 2012). Currently, responsibilities for gender policy are
assigned within the Ministry of Law and Gender.

Key informants from various ministries interviewed by the study team noted
that, theoretically, this fluidity could have had positive ramifications because,
through the changes, multiple ministries have gained exposure to gender issues.
In reality, uncertainty about where the gender policy platform should reside
has reduced political commitment and accountability to gender equality.
Consequently, it has been difficult to sustain programs, advocacy, and policies in
support of gender equality.

Maldives' Delay in Achieving MDG 3

Maldives is on track to achieve five of the eight MDGs. However, despite its relatively progressive civil law and public efforts to counter gender-discriminatory
provisions of Sharia law, the country is lagging in its achievement of MDG3—
promoting women's empowerment and gender equality (Ministry of Finance and
Treasury and UNDP 2014).[5] A lack of capacity in local and national public
institutions hinders implementation of gender-sensitive laws, policies, and programs; and staff rarely mainstreams gender issues into daily operations. Additional
challenges include limited budget allocations, low awareness of gender issues, and
lack of capacity among civil society organizations addressing gender inequality to
engage and influence government policy (ADB 2014).

Maldives' Economic Development

The World Bank's recent Systematic Country Diagnostic (SCD) for Maldives
describes in detail the noninclusive nature of Maldives' economic development
model (World Bank 2015). Here we focus specifically on the challenges and
opportunities that the Maldivian economic development process offers for
gender equality.

One key challenge is in women's employment opportunities. Over the past
decade, modernization and mechanization of traditional sectors, such as fishing,
have not taken into account the roles of women. While men own the boats and
catch the fish, women have traditionally been responsible for post-harvesting
activities, such as drying, salting, and preserving fish. Increased development and
tourism have contributed to an increase in the demand for fish. In response, the

fishing industry has been modernized, and mechanization has largely taken over fish-processing activities. Thus women's work has been phased out. However, there have been minimal—if any—efforts to support them in building alternative livelihoods (ADB 2014).

In the more recently developed sectors of the economy, gender differentials also abound. Tourism is one such sector. Tourism has grown rapidly and could offer employment opportunities for women. However, there are significantly fewer women than men employees in tourism because this sector has not fully taken into account the particular social constraints of, opportunities for, and training needs of women who are interested in finding employment in this area. In another example, the Maldivian government has identified micro, small, and medium enterprises (MSMEs) as a key aspect of its economic development agenda. However, most commercially viable ventures appear to be dominated by male entrepreneurs, with few female entrepreneurs, especially on more remote islands and atolls.

Maldives' pattern of economic development also has potentially negative ramifications for the large youth population, particularly young men. Rapid economic growth over the last few decades has fueled aspirations that are unrealistic in the context of the limitations of a small, island economy and that the "new" Maldivian economy thus far has not been able to fulfill. At the same time, massive subsidization of daily necessities and the cultural acceptance of one family member supporting all have contributed to decreased urgency among youth to find a job (World Bank 2014). The result has been a high number of idle youth—particularly young men—who are neither employed nor pursuing an education or training (also termed NEET for "not in employment, education, or training").[6] Chapter 3 below explores how this situation may fuel gender-specific risks for young men's lives.

Informal Institutions: Politics, Society, Culture, and Religion

Maldives' legal, institutional, and economic developments have been part of an unprecedented period of social, political, and religious transformation in the country, summarized in box 2.1. Shifts in migration, urbanization, structure of the home and family, religious conservatism, and a youth disconnect are all characteristics of this period of transformation that influence current and potential future gender equality in the country.

Migration, Urbanization, and the Structure of the Home and Family
Family structure in Maldives is shifting toward more rigidly defined gender roles. Traditional family structure was relatively fluid in terms of roles and spaces allowed to men and women. In fact, Maldivian homes were built in a way that facilitated interaction among men and women in private and public spaces. Homes were large and open in design, with many women's jobs—such as cooking or cleaning fish—taking place in public spaces outside of the home compound. Thus, historically there was little that contributed to the lack of a strict divide

Box 2.1 Changing Culture and Society in Maldives in the 21st Century

Until the mid-20th century, Maldives was a relatively quiet backwater, largely ignored by the rest of the world and with life continuing as it had for generations. Tourism started increasing in the 1980s, but it was arguably the devastation wrought on Maldives by the 2004 tsunami and the consequent flood of development aid that propelled Maldives to the forefront of the world's attention. Rapid economic development further opened up the country to the outside world, and ideas and norms from the rest of the world flooded Maldivian society. The country became known as a tourist haven. By some estimates, in 2009 more than 600,000 tourists—twice the population of the country—visited Maldives, and by 2013 the number had increased to over 1 million (Ministry of Tourism 2014). The internationalization of the country has also meant an increased inflow of expatriate labor, as well as the entry of Islamic groups from other parts of South Asia and the Middle East. All are bringing their cultures and ideals to the social development of Maldives.

A rise in internal migration fueled by Maldives' economic development has added to the mixing of cultural and social norms. Most inter-atoll migration is from the outer atolls to Malé. According to data from the 2014 census, the population growth rate of Malé between the 2006 and 2014 censuses stands at almost 3 percent (2.96 percent), compared to an intercensus average growth rate of 0.78 percent in all other atolls combined, and a national average of 1.6 percent (Ministry of Planning and National Development 2015).

between private and public roles for women. Women played an important role in family, politics, and society and led a life with few restrictions. With the increasing urbanization and migration to the bigger atolls and Malé that is accompanying Maldives' economic growth, the very structure of housing has changed. Homes have gone from being large, open spaces to small, closed spaces with a clear divide between the internal and external, the private and public. Anthropological studies suggest that this change has contributed to greater spatial concentration and isolation for women (Fulu 2014).

Growing Religious Conservatism

An increasingly conservative form of Islam in Maldives is further influencing changes in gender roles and expectations in ways that disadvantage women in both private and public spheres. Islam in Maldives has not historically been conservative. In fact, the traditional form of Islam practiced in Maldives was a unique model of tolerance that incorporated preexisting cultural practices while adhering to religious Islamic scriptures (Roul 2013). Maldives also historically had more gender-egalitarian social norms than other South Asian countries. For instance, unlike the rest of South Asia, arranged marriage has been relatively rare, couples may reside with either maternal or paternal parents after marriage (depending on space and practicality rather than any social prescriptions), and divorce practices are fluid and easy. There has also been a strong cultural emphasis on maintaining a peaceful equilibrium between men and women in the home and in society. Also unlike other South Asian countries, the traditional Maldivian notion of masculinity has encompassed peace and nonviolence (Fulu 2014).

From about the 1990s, the situation started shifting and a more conservative stream of Islam has increasingly gained favor, with concomitant detrimental effects on gender equality. Some anthropological research suggests that this stricter interpretation of Islam and resultant social conservatism are a reaction to perceived negative impacts of globalization on Maldivian society and a way to propose an alternate view of what the "new" Maldives should look like (Amir 2011; Fulu 2014). Research also suggests that a schism is growing between the extremely liberal and increasingly conservative (Amir 2011). Consequently, the space for balanced discussion and debate that could help ameliorate the situation is shrinking. Young men and women may be particularly vulnerable to the appeal of the conservative values triggered by a stricter interpretation of Islam, in ways that make gender roles more rigid and less equitable.

Increasing Youth Disconnect

These social, familial, economic, and political changes occurring rapidly and simultaneously have left young Maldivians searching for a new identity, as traditional practices and professions clash with new ideas. There are, however, few—if any—role models who can demonstrate how to bridge the family traditions of the older generation with the more recently globalized views of youth in the new Maldives. Although a small group of youth is thriving in the current national context, many are struggling: they face the shackles of the limited island economy and a lack of empowerment, social support, and community engagement, together with a reliance on their family's income and the limitations therein. One particularly worrisome aspect of these dynamics is the disconnect between the available economic opportunities in high-growth sectors, and young Maldivians' often-unrealistic preference for different, white-collar jobs that don't exist in sufficient quantity. Thus, existing jobs are filled by foreign labor, adding to Maldivian youth's disconnect and disengagement. Finally, youth in Maldives today are contending with increasingly gendered shifts in family structure and conservative religious values and face an education and training system that ill prepares them for the new economy (World Bank 2014).

In conclusion, as a result of both the apparent contradiction between the old and the new and the perception among Maldivian youth of a lack of acceptable opportunities for education and work, young people are growing increasingly disconnected from family and society and the related, traditional identities that defined their transition to adulthood (World Bank 2014). In this gap, the conservative views and role models espoused by a stricter interpretation of Islam may be appealing as an alternate anchor, and one that is likely to be detrimental to young people's views on gender roles and gender-egalitarian behavior (figure 2.4).

The youth disconnect is an important theme in the story of gender inequality in the Maldives. Very similar contextual conditions contribute to

Figure 2.4 Dynamics of Youth Disconnect in Maldives

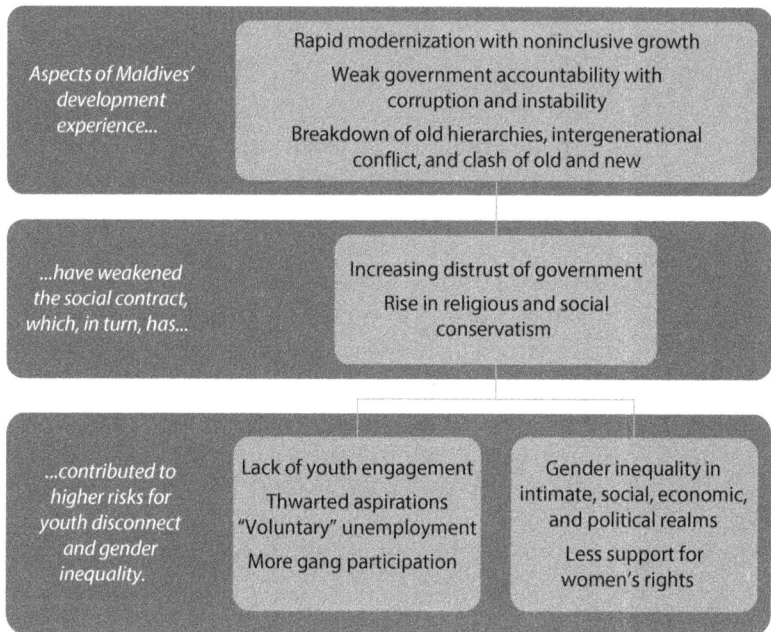

higher risks for youth and worsening gender inequality (figure 2.4). In particular, youth disengagement and higher gender inequality both have likely been exacerbated by those aspects of the Maldivian development model that have triggered a breakdown in the social contract between the government and its citizens. Further, the demographics of the Maldives makes youth disconnect critical for gender inequality: youth make up a large proportion of the country. Young men who do not find a role in their society at large may well turn to redefining their roles within their homes so as to exert greater control to make up for their social disconnectedness. We turn in the next chapter to the implications for gender differentials in the public and private spheres of life.

Notes

1. "The biggest and the most serious threat to the infant democracy in Maldives is corruption," said Maldives' auditor general according to a recent news report: "Corruption: Serious Threat to Maldives Says Auditor General," Raajje.mv, November 3, 2014, https://raajje.mv/26880.

2. Malaysia, Indonesia, and Mauritius were countries nominated by Maldivian interviewees in this report as countries comparable to Maldives.

3. See "Maldives Must Empower Anti-corruption Commission, Says Transparency International," *Minivan News*, May 21, 2014, http://minivannews.com/politics/maldives-must-further-empower-anti-corruption-commission-concludes-transparency-international-85318#sthash.HYi7twfI.dpbs; "Comment: Getting Away with Murder,"

Minivan News, March 28, 2015, http://minivannews.com/politics/comment-getting
-away-with-murder-94278#sthash.DoB84Kxh.dpbs; "Comment: Imprisoning of
Former President Casts Doubt on Judiciary," *Minivan News*, March 21, 2015, http://
minivannews.com/politics/comment-imprisoning-of-former-president-casts-doubt-on
-judiciary-94184#sthash.ZSAZfbIU.dpbs; "Comment: Get Up, Stand Up," *Minivan
News*, March 11, 2015, http://minivannews.com/politics/comment-get-up-stand-up
-93199#sthash.0DnpWVlh.dpbs; and "Maldives: Beautiful, Corrupt and Slowly
Disappearing," *The Huffington Post*, March 24, 2015, http://www.huffingtonpost.ca
/capt-trevor-greene/maldives-president-prison_b_6928812.html.

4. See "Maldives Girl Repeatedly Raped by Her Father Is Sentenced to 100 Lashes after
Admitting Adultery with Another Man," *The Huffington Post*, February 27, 2013.
http://www.huffingtonpost.co.uk/2013/02/27/maldives-girl-raped-father-sentenced
-100-lashes-adultery-_n_2772213.html; and "The Culture of Flogging in Maldives:
A Systematic Abuse of Human Rights," *Minivan News*, March 25, 2013. http://
minivannews.com/politics/the-culture-of-flogging-in-the-maldives-a-systematic
-abuse-of-human-rights-55092#sthash.ZMHToYQy.dpuf.

5. This issue is also an important focus of Maldives National Reproductive Health
Strategy 2014–2018 (http://www.searo.who.int/maldives/mediacentre/nrhs-2014
-2018.pdf).

6. The concept of NEET refers to the share of youth who are neither in employment nor
in education or training in the youth population and is a relatively new concept that
is intended to allow for a deeper and more nuanced examination of youth inactivity
and exclusion than would the narrower indicators of employment or labor force
participation. However, there are multiple definitions of NEET and data are scarce:
thus we do not use this indicator as a measure in this report.

References

ADB (Asian Development Bank). 2007. "Maldives: Gender and Development Assessment."
Strategy and Program Assessment, Asian Development Bank, Mandaluyong City,
Philippines. http://www.adb.org/documents/maldives-gender-and-development
-assessment.

———. 2014. *Maldives—Gender Equality Diagnostic of Selected Sectors*. Mandaluyong City,
Philippines: Asian Development Bank.

Al Suood, Husnu. 2014. *The Maldivian Legal System*. Malé, Maldives: Maldives Law
Institute.

Amir, Hassan. 2011. "Islamism and Radicalism in Maldives." Masters Thesis, Naval
Postgraduate School, Monterey, CA. http://calhoun.nps.edu/bitstream/handle
/10945/10724/11Dec_Amir.pdf?sequence=1.

Department of National Planning, Republic of Maldives. 2012. *ICPD Beyond 2014:
Maldives Operational Review 2012—Progress, Challenges and Way Forward*. Malé,
Maldives: Government of Maldives.

Fulu, Emma. 2014. *Domestic Violence in Asia: Globalization, Gender and Islam in Maldives*.
London: Routledge.

Government of Maldives. n.d. *Maldives National Reproductive Health Strategy 2014–2018*.
http://www.searo.who.int/maldives/mediacentre/nrhs-2014-2018.pdf.

Hope for Women. 2012. *Maldives NGO Shadow Report to the Committee on the Elimination
of Discrimination against Women, 2012*. Malé, Maldives: Hope for Women.

Institute of Social Studies Trust. 2008. *Progress of Women in South Asia 2007*. New Delhi: UNIFEM South Asia Office.

Ministry of Finance and Treasury and UNDP (United Nations Development Programme) in Maldives. 2014. *Maldives Human Development Report 2014—Bridging the Divide: Addressing Vulnerability, Reducing Inequality*. Malé, Maldives: Ministry of Finance and Treasury and the United Nations Development Programme in Maldives.

Ministry of Health and Gender, Republic of Maldives. 2014. *Maldives Health Profile 2014*. Government of Maldives. http://www.health.gov.mv/publications/13_1395305886 _Maldives_Health_Profile_2014_final_final.pdf.

Ministry of Human Resources, Youth and Sport, Republic of Maldives. n.d. "Maldives 2008 Employment Act." Unofficial English translation obtained by the ILO. http:// www.ilo.org/dyn/natlex/natlex4.detail?p_lang=en&p_isn=85764&p_count =96150&p_classification=01.02&p_classcount=1071 and http://www.ilo.org/dyn /natlex/docs/ELECTRONIC/85764/96218/F1772069692/MDV85764%20English .pdf.

Ministry of Planning and National Development. 2015. *Population and Housing Census 2014*. Statistical Release 1: Population and Households. http://statisticsmaldives.gov .mv/nbs/wp-content/uploads/2015/10/Census-Summary-Tables1.pdf

Ministry of Tourism, Republic of Maldives. 2014. *Tourism Yearbook 2014*. Malé, Maldives: Government of Maldives (accessed April 15, 2015), http://tourism.gov.mv /downloads/2014dec/tourism%20year%20book%202014.pdf.

Roul, Animesh. 2013. "The Threat from Rising Extremism in Maldives." *CTC Sentinel* 6 (3): 24–28. https://www.ctc.usma.edu/posts/the-threat-from-rising-extremism-in-the -maldives.

Shareef, Mizna. n.d. *Unofficial Translation of the Domestic Violence Act, Act Number 3/2012*. Conducted on behalf of UNFPA (accessed April 19, 2015), http://countryoffice .unfpa.org/filemanager/files/maldives/the_domestic_violence_act_2012_maldives _english_translation_unofficial.pdf.

Solotaroff, Jennifer L., and Rohini Prabha Pande. 2014. *Violence against Women and Girls: Lessons from South Asia*. South Asia Development Forum. Washington, DC: World Bank. https://openknowledge.worldbank.org/handle/10986/20153.

Transparency International. 2011. *Transparency International Corruption Perceptions Index 2011* (accessed March 26, 2015), http://www.transparency.org/cpi2011/results.

———. 2013. *Transparency Maldives Global Corruption Barometer Survey 2013* (accessed March 26, 2015), http://transparency.mv/wp-content/uploads/2013/12/FINAL-TM -POSTER-ENG.pdf.

UNDP (United Nations Development Programme). 2011. *Women in Public Life in Maldives: A Situational Analysis*. Malé, Maldives: UNDP.

UN Women (United Nations Entity for Gender Equality and the Empowerment of Women) and UNDP (United Nations Development Programme). 2014. *Maldivian Women's Vision Document*. Malé, Maldives: UNDP.

WHO (World Health Organization). 2013. *WHO Country Cooperation Strategy: Republic of Maldives 2013–2017*. WHO Country Office for Maldives. http://www.who.int /countryfocus/cooperation_strategy/ccs_mdv_en.pdf.

World Bank. 2014. *Youth in Maldives: Shaping a New Future for Young Women and Men through Engagement and Empowerment.* Washington, DC: World Bank. http://documents.worldbank.org/curated/en/2014/10/23922488/youth-maldives -shaping-new-future-young-women-men-through-engagement-empowerment.

———. 2015. *Maldives—Systematic Country Diagnostic: Identifying Opportunities and Constraints to Ending Poverty and Promoting Shared Prosperity.* Washington, DC: World Bank. http://documents.worldbank.org/curated/en/2015/11/25479516 /maldives-identifying-opportunities-constraints-ending-poverty-promoting-shared -prosperity-systematic-country-diagnostic.

CHAPTER 3

Gender Differentials in Outcomes

Introduction

Recent shifts in identity, gender roles, and social norms and increasing conservatism are affecting gender differentials in the private and public spheres of agency, endowments, and opportunities (figure 3.1). On the one hand, research shows that gender inequalities in basic well-being (in health and education) are largely diminished in Maldives, thanks in part to health and education systems. On the other hand, other social and cultural restrictions on women persist and may be expanding, influencing gender equality, in particular, in the private realm.

Gender Differentials in the Private Sphere: Agency

We consider three categories of indicators of agency that measure gender differentials in domestic relations (the private sphere): (1) decision making in the household, (2) access to and ownership of household economic and financial resources, and (3) vulnerability to violence. While in themselves these are important indicators of gender equality, they are also significant because they can have secondary effects on gender differentials for outcomes in the public sphere, for example affecting women's access to education, political participation, and employment opportunities.

Decision Making in the Household

Household decision making appears to be relatively gender-egalitarian in Maldives. A nationally representative sample of married women surveyed by Maldives' 2009 Demographic and Health Survey (DHS) found that husband and wife make most household decisions jointly (MOHF and ICF Macro 2010; see figure 3.2). Data from the same DHS on men's attitudes on decision making echo this: most surveyed husbands agree that most household decisions should be made jointly.

Figure 3.1 World Development Report Modified Framework—Focus on Outcomes

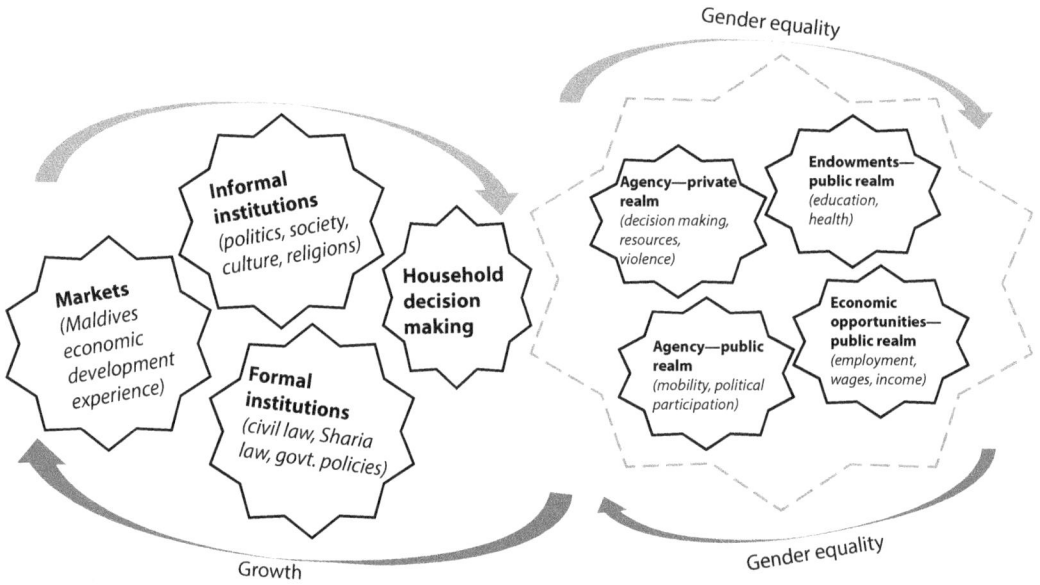

Figure 3.2 Women's Reports of Decision Making in the Household

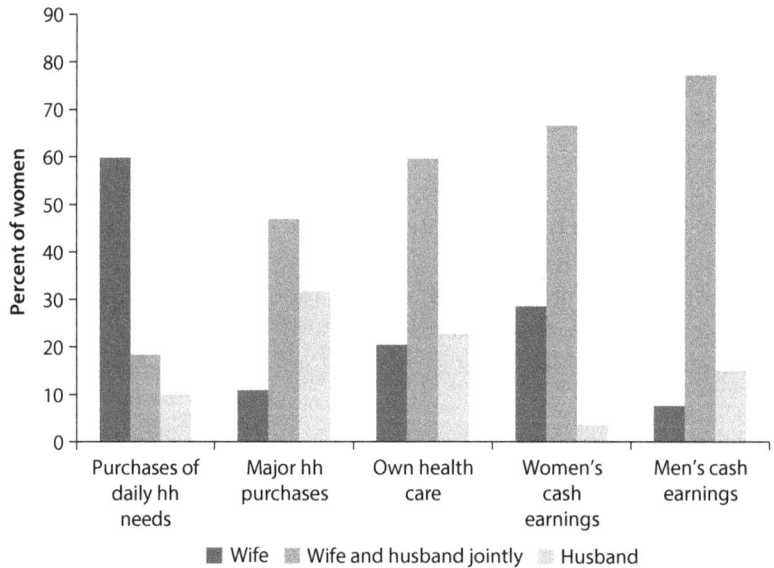

Source: MOHF and ICF Macro 2010.
Note: hh = household.

Ownership of Household Economic and Financial Resources

Ownership and control of household assets in Maldivian families squarely advantages men. Few women own property, for instance. According to the 2006 Maldives' Census, only 31.3 percent of recorded homeowners were women, and men and women jointly owned only 3.1 percent of homes—in stark contrast to 65.5 percent of male sole owners (figure 3.3) (Ministry of Planning and National Development 2008). This statistic is in part due to gender-differentiated property ownership rights under Sharia law that disadvantage women and in part likely reflects that men are the main decision makers about ownership of household assets and resources. Key informants interviewed in February 2015 reaffirmed the gender disparity in land ownership.

Recent studies show that home ownership is also skewed away from women in other countries in South Asia and in Latin America. A study using Living Standards Measurement Study data from six Latin American countries (Deere, Alvarado, and Tywman 2012) found that women were less likely to own homes than men in all six countries, especially in Paraguay (35 percent of women owned homes in 2001) and Guatemala (27 percent in 2000). Similarly, a recent survey in Karnataka state, India, found that about 24 percent of women owned their own homes versus 75 percent of men (Swaminathan, Lahoti, and Suchitra 2012).

Women in Maldives also rarely own key means of transportation, which are critical assets in Maldives' economy because of the lack of affordable and efficient public transportation options within and between atolls. Nationwide (figure 3.3), women own only about 20 percent of all registered vehicles, including battery-powered scooters, motorcycles, cars, and other vehicles (ADB 2014).

Figure 3.3 Gender Differentials in Ownership of Assets and Resources

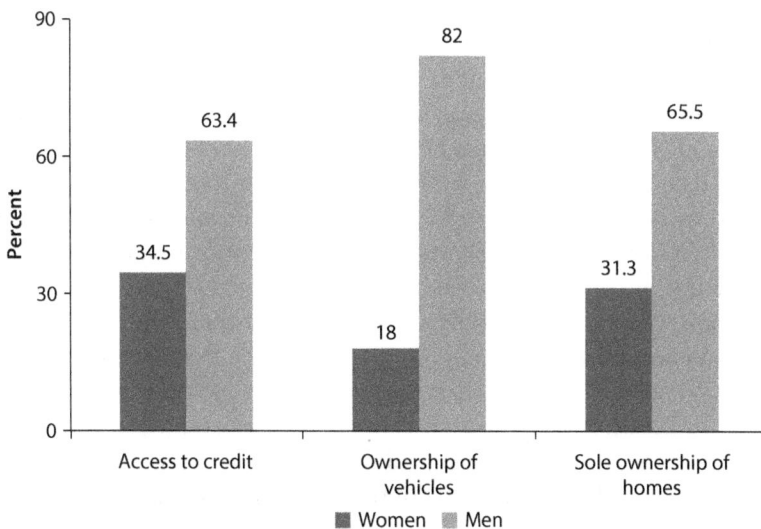

Sources: ADB 2014; Ministry of Planning and National Development 2007.

Inequality is even starker in the atolls; women own 13.8 percent of vehicles in the atolls, as opposed to 24 percent of vehicles in Malé.[1] Boats used for fishing or interisland travel are owned almost entirely by men (ADB 2014). This lack of access to affordable and reliable transport impedes women's abilities to engage in commercial and other income-generating activities (ADB 2014).

Because of their limited ownership of assets—including homes or means of transportation—women lack the collateral needed to secure credit from banks, (figure 3.3) therefore impeding their ability to finance business ventures (ADB 2014). The country's 2009–2013 National Strategic Action Plan recommended that the government provide women with self-help grants for small and medium-sized enterprises and promote microcredit programs to help bridge this gender gap (ADB 2014). However, the extent to which this has been implemented is unclear.

Women's Vulnerability to Gender-Based Violence

In 2006, the most recent year for which nationally representative data on violence against women are available, almost 20 percent (19.5 percent) of Maldivian women reported that they had experienced some form of intimate partner violence, be it physical or sexual or both (Fulu 2006). This partner violence rate is lower than that of several other countries in the region, including Nepal at 28.2 percent (MOHP, New ERA, and ICF International Inc. 2012), India at 37.2 percent (International Institute for Population Sciences and Macro International 2007), and Bangladesh at 53.3 percent (NIPORT, Mitra and Associates, and Macro International 2009).

Overall violence, by partners or nonpartners, has a similar prevalence. According to data from the DHS and other sources, over one-quarter (28.4 percent) of Maldivian women have experienced physical or sexual violence at some point in their lives by either partners or nonpartners. Although this proportion is lower than in other South Asian countries, it is higher than in comparable middle-income Asian countries like Malaysia, Indonesia, or the Philippines (figure 3.4).[2] Consistent with global trends, younger Maldivian women are at a higher risk of partner violence than are older women (Fulu 2007a).

Women in Maldives are aware of and concerned about their risks of gender-based violence not just within the house but also in public spaces. In a study conducted in 2012 by the United Nations Development Programme (UNDP) with over 1,000 women, the majority of survey respondents named gender-based violence as one of their major concerns (UN Women and UNDP 2014). Women's concern and experience of violence continues despite the passage of the Domestic Violence Prevention Act in 2012. Evidence from Maldives and other countries documents well the harmful effects that violence has on women's health (Fulu 2006). A large body of research across South Asia shows that the threat of violence can hamper girls' and women's school attendance, labor force participation, and achievement of six of the eight Millenium Development Goals (MDGs), as well as a country's overall development progress (Solotaroff and Pande 2014).

Figure 3.4 Reported Lifetime Partner/Nonpartner Physical or Sexual Violence

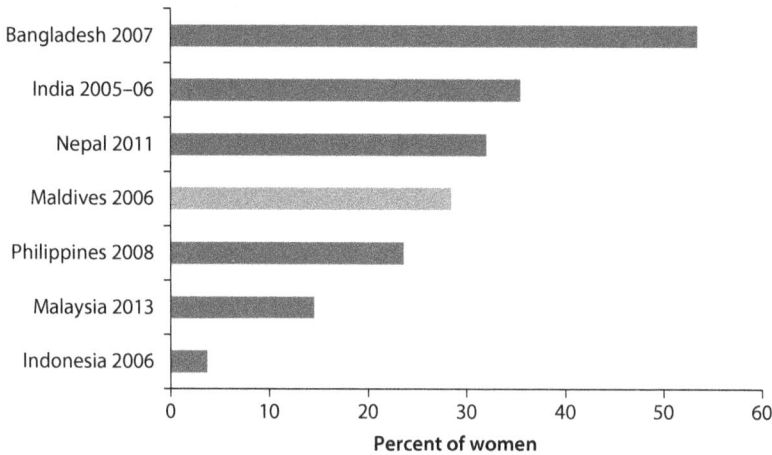

Source: DHS and other national data compiled by UN Women; Shuib et al. 2013.

Gender Differentials in the Public Sphere: Agency

This section reviews three categories of indicators of agency that measure gender differentials in the public sphere: (1) mobility outside of the home, (2) political participation and voice in society, and (3) violence in the public sphere.

Mobility Outside of the Home

While casual observation of public spaces (roads, public transportation, and so on) in Maldives suggests that there are little to no barriers to women's mobility, key informant interviews and others' research (UNDP 2011) reveal that women face a disadvantage for certain types of mobility, such as interisland mobility. For instance, parents are hesitant to allow young female family members to travel to other islands for tertiary education or for jobs such as those located on resort islands as part of the tourism sector. Consequently, there are fewer young women than men enrolled in tertiary education programs and employed in tourism. Curbs on women's mobility may be further exacerbated by women's limited ownership and control of transportation means.

Political Participation and Voice in Society

Women in Maldives participate actively in the political process at the grassroots, in campaigns for political candidates running for office, or at rallies. However, this does not translate into visible official political participation. In fact, women's participation in leadership positions is low at local and national levels (Ritchie, Rogers, and Sauer 2014).

At the island and atoll levels, government-appointed island and community chiefs have historically been responsible for economic development and religious activities (Fulu 2007b). Women are woefully underrepresented in this level of administration. Data from the latest census show that only 5.1 percent of island counselors are women, while 0.5 percent of atoll counselors and no city counselors are women (National Bureau of Statistics 2016, table 20.8). The introduction of women's development committees (WDCs) in 1982 created some opportunities for women's participation in community development. Unfortunately, opportunities presented to women through the WDCs tend to be relatively minor economic activities. For more significant endeavors, the women's committees frequently do not have the required budget (Ritchie, Rogers, and Sauer 2014). Outside of government structures, there are few opportunities for women to shape local agendas, in part because there are few nongovernmental organizations (NGOs) in the country that focus on women's issues (Fulu 2007b).

At the national level also, political participation among Maldivian women is limited. As of February 1, 2015, Maldives ranked 128th out of 190 countries across the globe with regard to female representation in parliament (Inter-Parliamentary Union, n.d.). Regionally, Maldives ranks near the bottom: as of 2014, Maldivian women held slightly less than 6 percent of seats in the national parliament (5.6 percent), which is the third lowest rate in the region after Bhutan (6.4 percent) and Sri Lanka (5.8 percent). Such figures stand in stark contrast to other countries in the region, such as Nepal and Afghanistan, where approximately 33 percent and 28 percent of parliamentarians are women, respectively (World Bank 2014a). Maldivian women's participation in national political life is hampered not only by social norms and familial attitudes that inhibit such participation but also by a lack of knowledge among women about political structures (UNDP 2011). In this situation, key informant interviews revealed that many of the women who do achieve high-ranking positions in government or within political parties are often from the political and economic minority elite and are not representative of the "average" Maldivian woman.

A recent UNDP report suggests that

> …while the benefits of participation of women is generally accepted, limited opportunities and information for women, and cultural barriers, restrict the choices available to them. In addition, limited resources, cultural barriers and in some cases conservative religious groups combine to restrict the participation and leadership of women in society, politics and decision making. (UNDP 2011, foreword)

Violence in the Public Sphere

Gender differentials in violence stem from the location and type of violence. Unlike the case with women, men are not particularly vulnerable to domestic violence but are vulnerable to violence in the public sphere, primarily related to gang activity. Young men under the age of 25 appear particularly at risk.

Historically, "gangs" in Maldives have been relatively benign groupings of males, most commonly under the age of twenty-five. Gangs can range in size from a few young men to hundreds. A study by the Asia Foundation in 2012 estimated that in Malé alone there were 20–30 active gangs at the time, with a membership of between 50 and 400 each. A majority of gang members interviewed in this same study admitted to having suffered from violence or having perpetrated violence. Moreover, the study reports that the intensity of gang violence has been on the rise, with knives and other weapons replacing fistfights (Asia Foundation and MIPSTAR 2012).

Gang violence is motivated by factors within the individual member, within the group, or by external parties. Four types of motivation are frequently cited: revenge for previous disputes, rivalries such as over girlfriends, competition for material goods as a status symbol, and self-preservation. Of growing concern, as noted in the Asia Foundation's report, is that young male gang members are being increasingly recruited to commit violence for political and business purposes. Compounding these problems is increasing illicit drug use among gang members, which, in turn, is fueling drug-related violence. That the nature of gang violence is a serious problem is well illustrated by a gang member interviewed in the Asia Foundation study, who said, "…Maldivian gang violence can be much more brutal and frequent [than violence in other countries' gangs] as this is a small community and people can't hide in places for that long" (Asia Foundation and MIPSTAR 2012, 8). Key informants interviewed by the study team reaffirmed these assertions, labeling gangs a serious social problem and source of risk for young Maldivian men.

Gender Differentials in the Public Sphere: Education and Health Endowments

Maldivian laws are unequivocal about gender equality in education and access to health. Sociocultural norms also do not discriminate in these domains: unlike much of South Asia, Maldivian families do not typically deny daughters basic education or health care. However, women and girls face limited opportunities for higher education and preventive health care.

Education

At first glance it appears that there are no gender differentials in education in Maldives. Maldives has achieved universal primary education for both girls and boys. Enrollment levels are high until the lower-secondary level, and gender differentials in enrollment are minimal through higher-secondary schooling. Trends over time indicate that, since at least 2005, female enrollment in primary, lower-secondary, and higher-secondary schooling has kept pace with or surpassed male enrollment (figure 3.5), in both Malé and the atolls.

Enrollment levels beyond higher-secondary schooling, while low, are limited for *both* girls and boys, at 18 percent and 16 percent for boys and girls, respectively. However, some—albeit limited—research suggests that girls have fewer opportunities than do boys to gain tertiary education abroad, primarily because of household norms that frown upon girls and young women living away from home (Chitrakar 2009). The most recent data also show that girls' participation

Figure 3.5 Gender Differentials in Educational Enrollment in Maldives

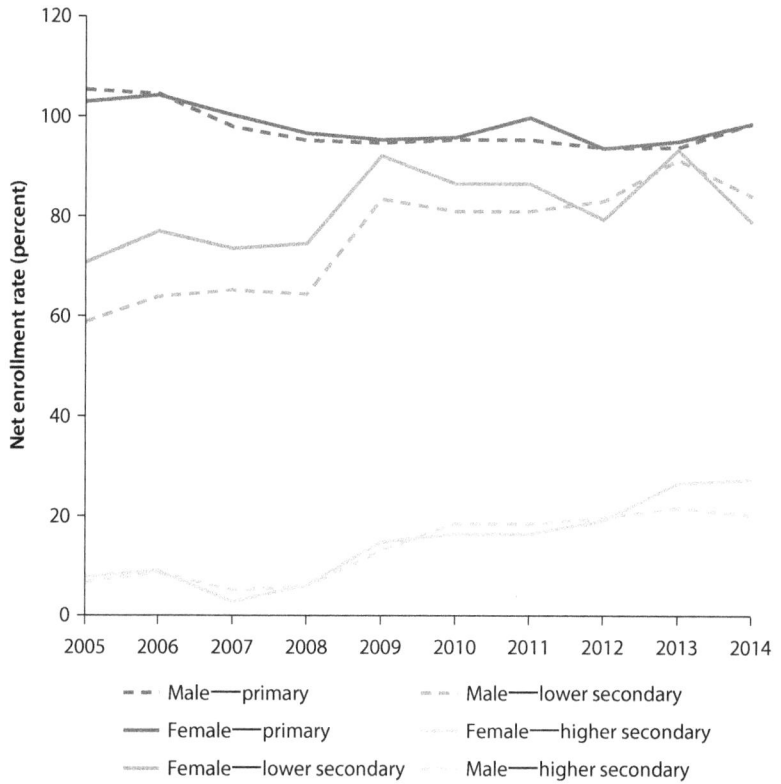

Source: Ministry of Education, n.d.

within the Maldives in postsecondary school technical education is practically nonexistent (National Bureau of Statistics 2016, table 7.22).

Disaggregation of national-level data reveals some gender differentials in education by residence and household poverty. Girls are at a disadvantage in poorer, rural areas. According to the 2009 DHS, girls are more likely than boys to be in school in urban areas but not in rural areas. In fact, rural girls are almost 60 percent more likely than rural boys to be neither in school nor working (figure 3.6). Girls in more remote atolls may also be at a disadvantage. Many islands are too small to allow for higher education institutions. Although quantitative data from Maldives' Ministry of Education do not reveal consistent patterns of gender differentials in higher schooling (Ministry of Education, n.d.), key informants interviewed for this report suggested that parents from smaller or outlying islands may be less willing to send daughters, compared to sons, to Malé to continue their higher or technical education.

Patterns in educational achievement follow a similar trajectory to those of enrollment. Girls fare as well as or better than boys through secondary school. For instance, data presented in figure 3.7 on the proportion of students between

Figure 3.6 Gender Differentials in Current Activity among Youth, by Residence

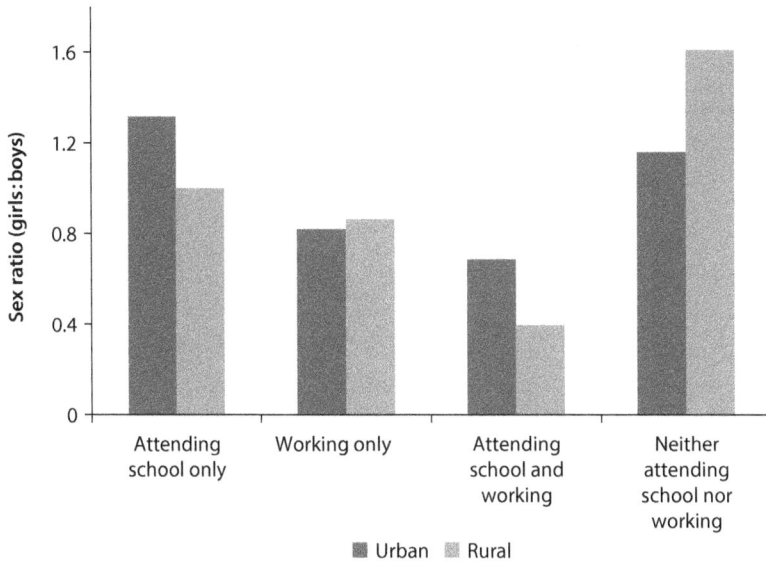

Source: MOHF and ICF Macro 2010.

Figure 3.7 Achievement in Higher Education, by Sex

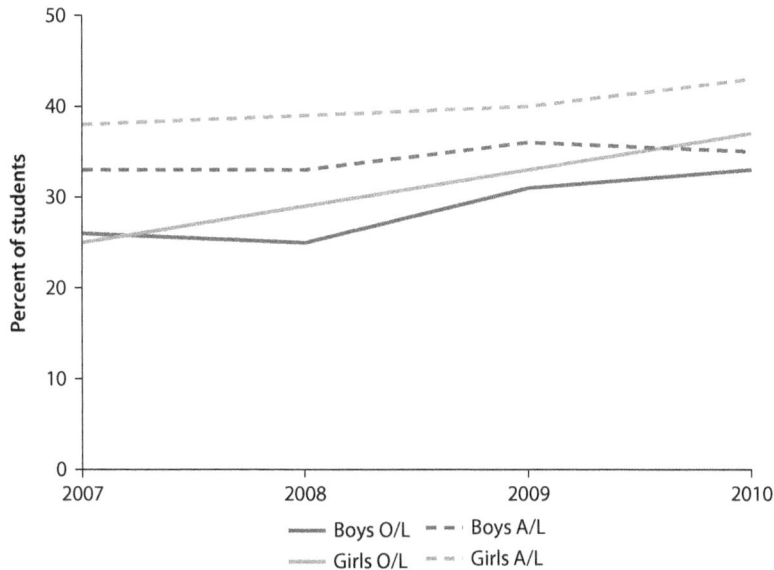

Source: World Bank 2012.
Note: A/L = advanced level (equivalent to 12th grade); O/L = ordinary level (equivalent to 10th grade).

2007 and 2010 who passed the general certificate of examinations ordinary level (GCE O/L, equivalent to 10th grade), or the GCE A/L (equivalent to 12th grade), show that a slightly higher proportion of girls were successful compared to boys (World Bank 2012). However, recent census data show that thereafter there is a wide gender gap in achievement through college and graduate education, with over 70 percent of bachelor, master, and doctoral level degrees awarded to boys, and 30 percent or less awarded to girls (Ministry of Planning and National Development 2015a).

Health and Mortality

Women and girls fare as well as or better than men and boys on multiple indicators of basic health. Unlike the rest of South Asia, Maldives does not exhibit gender differentials in childcare and mortality. Sex ratios at birth and in early childhood are egalitarian, and more than 90 percent of girls and boys are fully vaccinated. The overall incidence of malnutrition has declined, and sex differences for wasting have largely disappeared (Ministry of Planning and National Development 2004). In fact, current childhood malnutrition rates are slightly higher for boys than for girls (Ministry of Planning and National Development 2004). Female life expectancy is somewhat higher than that of males and has improved faster than has men's. Maternal mortality has also dropped rapidly over time. Broader reproductive health services are limited, but both men and women face these limitations (box 3.1).

A closer look reveals female nutritional disadvantage in adulthood. Main nutrition concerns for women include chronic anemia and zinc and vitamin A deficiencies (Ministry of Health and Gender 2014). The National Micronutrient Survey of 2007 (MOHF 2007) found that 15.4 percent of women of reproductive age were anemic and that more than one-third (38 percent) were iron deficient (Ministry of Health and Gender 2014). The reasons for high malnutrition among Maldivian women remain poorly understood. Certainly there are no legal restrictions in Sharia law. Maldivian families do not follow the feeding patterns of northern Indian households where women eat last and least. Perhaps the answers lie in a lack of awareness of the nutrition value (or lack thereof) of the types of food that women typically eat, particularly during pregnancy. More research is needed to determine the issues underlying this phenomenon.

Areas of health where men are disadvantaged include tobacco use and abuse of narcotic drugs. Almost half of all Maldivian men (45 percent) smoke compared with 12 percent of women, reflecting the highest levels of smoking in South Asia (Ministry of Health and Gender 2014). Drug use is particularly problematic among young men. A UN study revealed that 68 percent of surveyed youth identified drugs as a current challenge facing Maldivian youth (UNFPA 2005). The first-ever national survey on drug abuse in Maldives estimated current drug use in 2013 at 6.6 percent in Malé and 2 percent in the atolls, with the majority of drug use occurring among men 15–24 years of age (Asia Foundation and MIPSTAR 2012). There are links between such drug abuse and the gang membership described earlier. Drug abuse has negative

Box 3.1 Reproductive Health in Maldives: Lacking for Both Men and Women

Abortion is illegal in Maldives. In contrast, attitudes toward abortion are more liberal than the law: just over half of all men (57.5 percent) and two-thirds of all women (67.2 percent) respondents to a 2012 Human Rights Commission (HRC) study thought that women should have access to safe and legal abortion, at least in some circumstances (Human Rights Commission of Maldives 2012).

Birth control is legal, and almost 90 percent of men and women recently surveyed by the Maldivian HRC agreed that women should have access to birth control (Human Rights Commission of Maldives 2012). Yet, Maldives has surprisingly low contraceptive use given its low fertility rate and broad acceptance of contraceptive use. According to data from DHS surveys carried out in South Asian and some middle-income Southeast Asian countries around the same time as the 2009 Maldives DHS, Maldives has the second-lowest percent of currently married women who reported having ever used contraception (figure B3.1.1).

Overall, sexual and reproductive health services are limited for both young men and young women. Recent World Bank research found that there is a dearth of opportunities and venues for Maldivian youth—both girls and boys—to access information on sexual and reproductive health (World Bank 2014b). Data from the 2009 Maldives DHS show that a quarter of young men (21.9 percent) and young women (25.3 percent) talk to no one about reproductive health issues. Among those who do seek guidance, most seem to get their information from male and female friends rather than from a health professional, thus casting doubt on the accuracy of such information.

Figure B3.1.1 Women Reporting Having Ever Used Modern Contraception

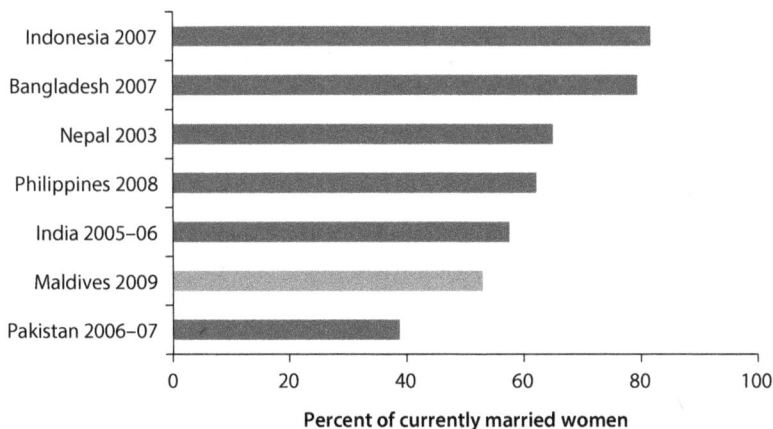

Source: Various DHS.

consequences for young men's employability, as a dearth of adequate rehabilitation services creates problems for convicted men when they seek employment and to reintegrate into society (Asia Foundation and MIPSTAR 2012; UNODC 2013). Poor reintegration following drug-related offenses may lead young men to seek social support by joining or rejoining gangs (World Bank 2014b). There is a strong law on narcotic drugs; but, according to our key informants, government de-addiction and rehabilitation centers do not provide adequate services.

Although drug users are overwhelmingly male, there is evidence to suggest that drug abuse is an increasing challenge for women. A UNDP (2004) report notes that "…many, if not most, young women involved in the criminal justice system had either been sentenced for drug offences or had committed other offences related to their drug use." Illicit drug use provides a set of unique challenges for women and girls because parents are more reluctant to publicly acknowledge their daughters' drug use, or to attempt to access services through the government-run Narcotics Control Board, than they are for sons (Alder and Polk 2004). Key informants for this study, and findings from other studies, note the need for gender-specific research and programs on drug abuse because girls and young women "…are often using drugs for different reasons to men, there are often differences in their drug use patterns and the ways in which they access drugs" (World Bank 2014b).

Gender Differentials in the Public Sphere: Employment and Income Opportunities

Female labor force participation is higher in Maldives than in other South Asian countries or other comparable middle-income countries. However, within Maldives, men are more likely to be employed than are women. As in many other countries in the developing world, women tend to be clustered in low-growth sectors and lower-paying positions than men, and women earn less than men. Demonstrating the dichotomous reality for women in Maldives, on paper they face no legal hurdles that could contribute to these employment differentials. Rather, household and personal beliefs about the social suitability or otherwise of certain kinds of training and jobs for women versus men, and gender unequal beliefs about men's and women's relative wages, are at play.

Labor Force Participation and Employment

According to data[3] from the World Development Indicators (World Bank 2014a), at 56 percent in 2013, female labor force participation[4] in Maldives is higher than in every South Asian country except Bhutan (66 percent) and Nepal (80 percent), and higher than that of comparable middle-income countries like Malaysia (44 percent) and Mauritius (44 percent). In contrast, the male labor force participation rate in Maldives is lower than male labor force participation in much of South Asia, though comparable to Malaysia (76 percent), Mauritius (74 percent), and Sri Lanka (76 percent).

Within Maldives, however, female labor force participation is lower than that of men at all age groups (figure 3.8), according to data from the 2009/10 Household Income and Expenditure Survey (HIES) (Department of National Planning, Statistics Division 2012). This gender gap is particularly pronounced between the ages of 20 and 24 years and between 50 and 54 years of age. The most recent labor force participation data from the 2014 census show that this pattern continues to persist (Ministry of Planning and National Development 2015b).

Unemployment data echo this theme: women are more likely to be unemployed than are men at most age groups starting from age 25–29 (figure 3.9). This female disadvantage holds regardless of the definition of unemployment, according to data and definitions used in the HIES 2009/10. Using the internationally comparable International Labour Organization (ILO) definition of unemployment,[5] between 2006 and 2010 Maldivian women's unemployment rose 8 percentage points, from 6 percent to 14 percent, whereas men's rose 6 percentage points, from 4 percent to 10 percent. Using a broader definition of unemployment that is particularly characteristic of Maldives, and that includes "discouraged workers,"[6] women's and men's unemployment rose 15 and 10 percentage points, respectively, between 2006 and 2010. By 2010, the broader unemployment rate for women stood at 39 percent, compared to 19 percent for men. The newly released 2014 census further modified the definition of unemployment used: "… to include only those who were seeking and available for work as unemployed" (Ministry of Planning and National Development 2015b). This modification

Figure 3.8 Age- and Sex-Specific Rate of Economic Activity

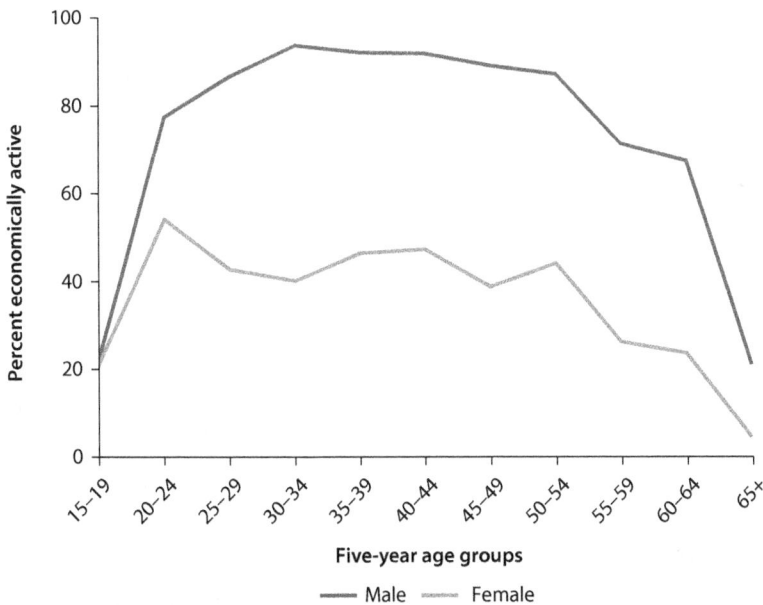

Source: Department of National Planning, Statistics Division 2012.

Figure 3.9 Unemployment Rate by Age and Gender

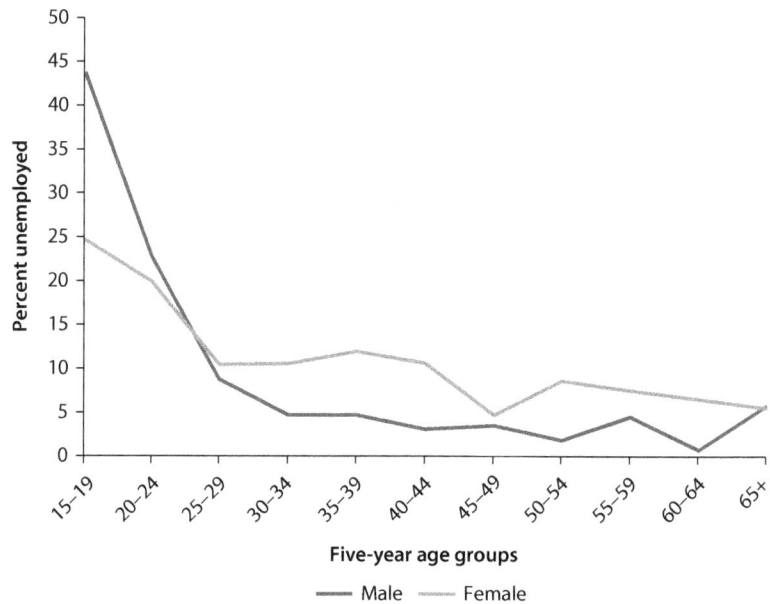

Source: Department of National Planning, Statistics Division 2012.

lowered unemployment rates for men and women, for 2006 and 2014. However, women still had a higher unemployment rate in 2014 (5.9 percent) than did men (4.9 percent).

Both men and women report a lack of opportunities on their resident island as their main reason for being unemployed. However, women—but not men—also cite the need to focus on childcare and household responsibilities as a reason for being unemployed, attesting to the societal expectations that they have to face through their reproductive years. According to data from the 2014 census, 13 percent of women and only 1 percent of men stated that they were unemployed because of household chores (figures 3.10 and 3.11, respectively) (Department of National Planning 2015b). This pattern illustrates how gender-unequal beliefs and roles in the private sphere (the importance of household chores for women but not men, for example) can disadvantage women's participation in the public sphere for reasons that men do not have to address.

Disaggregating by industry shows additional patterns of female disadvantage. Data from 2009/10 show that the most prominent, high-growth and high-employment sectors of the economy are male-dominated (figure 3.12). Men are more likely than women to be employed in industries such as fishing and quarrying; services such as electricity, gas, water, construction, wholesale and retail trade, tourism (hotel and restaurants), transport, storage, and communication; and public administration and defense. Women, on the other hand, tend to cluster in private household employment, education, health and social work, and manufacturing.

Figure 3.10 Women's Reported Reasons for Unemployment
percent

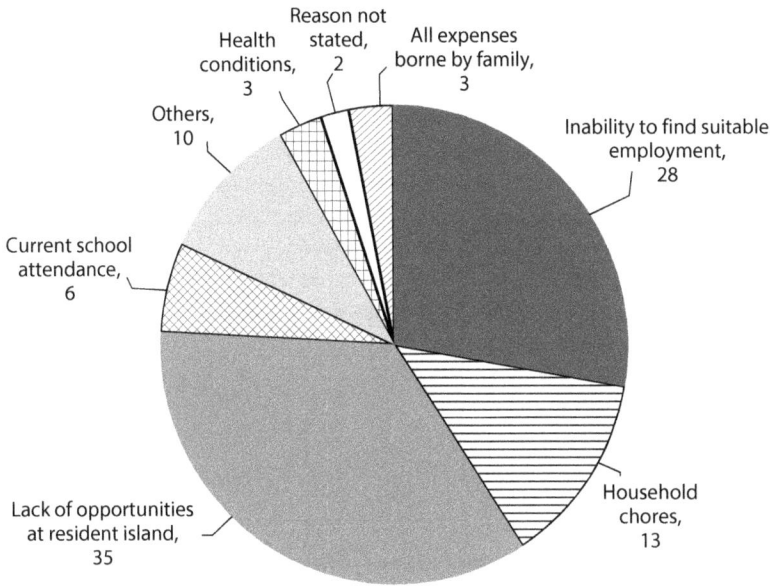

Reason not stated, 2
Health conditions, 3
All expenses borne by family, 3
Others, 10
Inability to find suitable employment, 28
Current school attendance, 6
Household chores, 13
Lack of opportunities at resident island, 35

Source: Ministry of Planning and National Development 2015b.

Figure 3.11 Men's Reported Reasons for Unemployment
percent

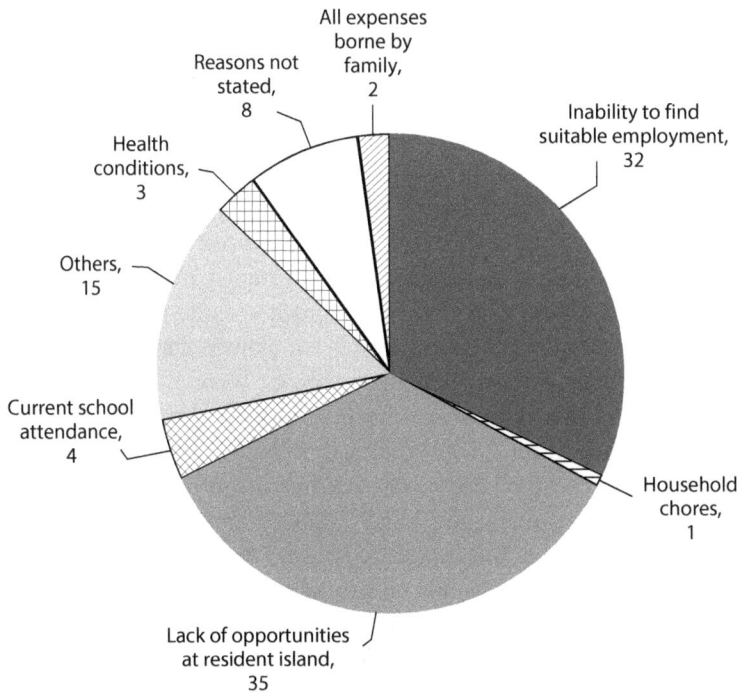

All expenses borne by family, 2
Reasons not stated, 8
Health conditions, 3
Inability to find suitable employment, 32
Others, 15
Current school attendance, 4
Household chores, 1
Lack of opportunities at resident island, 35

Source: Ministry of Planning and National Development 2015b.

Understanding Gender in Maldives • http://dx.doi.org/10.1596/978-1-4648-0868-5

Figure 3.12 Percent of Employees Who Are Women, by Industry

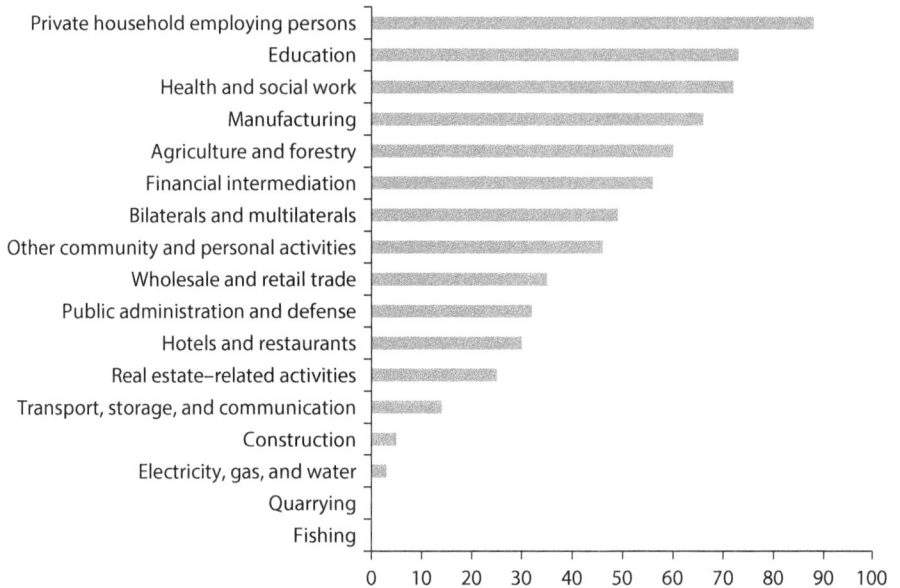

Source: ADB 2014; data for 2009/10.

Fishing is an important source of income for many Maldivians, yet women do not feature at all in the fishing sector. In fact, women used to play an important role in the value chain for fishing. However, as the fishing industry became increasingly mechanized, and since women did not own the key assets involved, their work became increasingly invisible and redundant (ADB 2014). The government continues to be the country's main employer, and, since 2008, women have comprised about half the civil service; however, they dominate in the "softer" ministries of health, family, and education. Men continue to dominate Maldives' tourism sector: 87 percent of the sector is comprised of men. In recent years, tourism has become an increasingly important part of the national economy, yet women continue to be left out. Women are often excluded because of social stigmas associated with young unmarried women staying on resort islands for significant periods of time, perceived risks of women traveling alone, high costs of transport, and limited childcare facilities for resort employees (International Trade Union Confederation 2009). Women dominate in the education and health sectors, probably because of the social acceptability of women as teachers and health providers. Interestingly, the HIES 2009/10 shows that manufacturing is also dominated by women, but it is not clear why this is the case.

Data from the 2014 census are unfortunately tabulated using a somewhat different categorization and thus not entirely comparable; however, these more recent data still show a majority of employees who are women in the same four industries: private household employment, education, health and social work, and manufacturing (Department of National Planning 2015b).

Income and Wages

The limited sex-disaggregated data on income in a report by ADB (2014) shows that for all industries, including those dominated by women, the average monthly earnings for women lag behind those of men. This difference in wages is most pronounced in the agriculture and forestry industry, where men earn 77.8 percent more than their female counterparts. Conservative religious norms, which reinforce a gendered division of labor, are often used to justify such wage gaps (ADB 2014). Further analysis controlling for gender differences in hours worked, skill levels, and other factors that also influence wages needs to be undertaken to establish the existence and extent of a gender wage gap. At the same time, policy makers need to recognize that certain gender-unequal social norms may inhibit women's opportunities to gain higher skills, work longer hours, and thus compete on an equal footing with men. Examples include social norms about acceptable training, hours worked, or permissible industries for women that are more restrictive than is the case for men. For inclusive labor market development, therefore, it is key to identify and address any such gender-biased factors so as to equalize labor income opportunities for women and men.

Lower incomes, combined with a limited control of household assets and productive resources, are particularly stringent issues for female-headed households.[7] More than half of all households in Maldives and more than 60 percent of households in Malé are female-headed households (Ministry of Planning and National Development 2007). A key reason for the large numbers of female-headed households is that men migrate for work. Although women do benefit from remittances, female-headed households still are somewhat likely to be poorer than households headed by men (ADB 2014; Ministry of Planning and National Development 2004). In the atolls, approximately one in three female-headed households fall below the poverty line compared to one in four male-headed households (Ministry of Planning and National Development 2004).

Youth Unemployment

Youth unemployment is a particularly problematic issue in Maldives for both men and women. In this problem Maldives is not alone: at a global level of 12.6 percent in 2013, youth unemployment is a growing concern worldwide. Globally, youth between the ages of 15 and 24 years are more than twice as likely as adults to be unemployed. Among world regions, South Asia has the lowest youth unemployment rate at 9.8 percent (ILO 2013). The youth unemployment rate of Maldives is higher than this regional average, at 12.4 percent as of the 2014 National Census (Ministry of Planning and National Development 2015b). Moreover, this number does not take into account the number of discouraged or idle youth (that is, those youth who are NEET, or not in employment, education, or training).

However, as illustrated by data from the 2009/10 HIES, gender differentials for youth unemployment are the reverse of those for adult unemployment. That is, unlike among adults, young men age 15–19 and 20–24 years are more likely to be unemployed than are young women in the same age groups (figure 3.13).

Figure 3.13 Youth Unemployment by Age, Sex, and Location

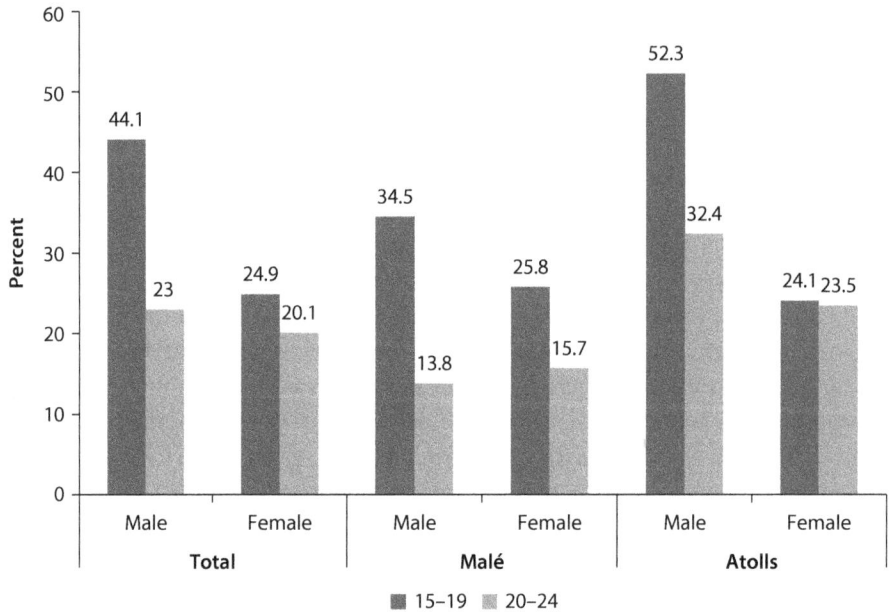

Source: Department of National Planning, Statistics Division 2012.

In the country as a whole, 44 percent of 15-to-19-year-old young men and almost a quarter of young women are unemployed. By age 20–24, unemployment drops somewhat but remains high at almost one-quarter of young men (23 percent) and one-fifth of young women (20.1 percent) unemployed. Young men of both young age groups are more likely to be unemployed in the atolls than in Malé. The situation is particularly dire for young men in the atolls, with more than half of those between the ages of 15 and 19 years being unemployed. One could argue that a notable proportion of these may be in school; however, even by age 20–24, a large one-third of young men in the atolls remain unemployed.

Norms, aspirations, and attitudes within the private sphere, as well as the lack of financial imperative to work, create a high reservation wage for Maldivian youth—men and women—that contributes to youth unemployment (World Bank 2014b). Other factors affecting both young men's and young women's employment include a low level of technical and "soft" skills among Maldivian youth that make them unappealing for employers and the ready availability of an expatriate workforce to take the place of unskilled local youth who have a high reservation wage despite their lack of skills. However, gender-specific constraints are also at play. Young women's employment is adversely affected by the norm that care of the home and family is their primary role in society. Social norms about the suitability of certain sectors for young women also contribute to their unemployment. The availability of expatriate women workers removes

---

Box 3.2 Gangs and Unemployment among Young Maldivian Men

A male disadvantage exists in unemployment among youth between the ages of 15 and 24 in Maldives. Participation in gangs is one key contributor. Gang participation incentivizes young men to earn income through informal sectors and to eschew engaging in the formal sector. A notable proportion of young men in gangs are engaged in buying and selling of drugs, through which they earn significantly more than they would if they were employed in the formal sector. As a respondent in an Asia Foundation study of gangs in Malé noted: "…the salary for people who have just left school (maybe MRF 2500 or $164 per month) is not sufficient to maintain their lifestyle. A single contract job undertaken as a member of the gang would earn them a much higher income than a monthly salary. This is easy money and they do not have to be at the office for 8–10 hours" (Asia Foundation and MIPSTAR 2012).

More broadly, the mere existence of gangs frequented by some young men seems to decrease the employability of all young men. Employers are reluctant to hire anyone who is, was, or could be a member of a gang. Reasons are likely twofold. First, gangs are illegal. Gang members face the risk of being detained by the police—almost two-thirds of gang members in Malé interviewed by the Asia Foundation in 2012 admitted to having been detained by police at least once. The law allows potential employers to access police records, and such a record can bar an applicant from being employable for five years. Second, employers may be reluctant to hire a young man suspected of having belonged to a gang, even without a police record, because of the characteristics associated with gang membership, namely, violence, drug use, and lack of responsibility.

Source: Asia Foundation and MIPSTAR 2012.

---

any incentives for employers to advocate for changing social norms that constrain young Maldivian women's employment in particular sectors. Young men's employment is adversely affected by the alternate income generation and social membership provided by gangs, which also negatively affect their potential formal employment (box 3.2).

Economic Insecurity for Women at Older Ages

Maldives currently has a pension system for retirees and the elderly, with benefits scaled relative to the earnings of an individual. When women in prime working ages are less likely to be represented in higher paying jobs—either because they earn less or because they have to forfeit certain jobs because of conflicts with their roles in the household—they benefit less from such a pension system than do men. Various pension schemes run by the national Maldives Pension Administration Office (MPAO) have a hugely unbalanced gender ratio, with 72 percent male and 28 percent female subscription in 2012 (Hope for Women 2012). More recent reports show that among all age groups women make up only about one-third of retirement savings account holders (MPAO 2013, 3), and

44 percent of beneficiaries of all pension schemes combined (National Bureau of Statistics 2016). These differentials have repercussions for women's economic situations in their old age.

Decline in Support for Gender Equality

Research conducted for this report and secondary literature reviewed indicate that popular support for gender equality is on the decline in Maldives. Surveys conducted by the Maldivian HRC in 2005 and 2011 show that the drop in support manifests in both urban and rural areas, and on all surveyed spheres of life, except for support in urban areas for women's right to divorce. Respondents from the key informant interviews conducted for this study, as well as other researchers (Fulu 2014; Roul 2013), suggest that a key factor in this eroding support is the spread of a more conservative interpretation of Islam that relegates women to the sphere of the household and that condones other gender-unequal social norms that disadvantage women.

Decline in Support for Women's Rights in Conjugal Relations

Men appear to be getting more conservative than women toward women's rights and gender equality: men became less supportive of women's rights across most of the statements illustrated in table 3.1 (Human Rights Commission of Maldives 2012).

For some outcomes, however, men and women both increasingly support patriarchal norms for the intimate relationships between women and men. Thus, between 2005 and 2011, men and women both have become more likely to agree that a "good wife always obeys her husband even if she disagrees," that women are obliged never to refuse their husbands sex, and that spousal violence

Table 3.1 Changes in Gender Differences in Attitudes toward Gender Equality, by Sex of Respondent and Year

Indicator	Percent of women strongly agreeing		Percent of men strongly agreeing	
	2005	2011	2005	2011
A good wife always obeys her husband even if she disagrees	44.8	52.4	35.4	43.9
It is important for a man to show his wife who is the boss	38.6	26.3	38.4	27.4
It is a wife's obligation to have sex with her husband even if she doesn't feel like it	20.8	33.3	16	26.8
If a man mistreats his wife, others outside the family should intervene	39.2	19.9	41.4	20.4
A women should be able to choose her friends even if her husband disapproves	18.4	13.2	18.2	12.2
A man should never hit his wife	30.8	39.7	35.1	29.9

Source: Human Rights Commission of Maldives 2012, tables on pages 44, 45, and 48.

Figure 3.14 Agreement with Statement "A Man Should Never Hit His Wife"

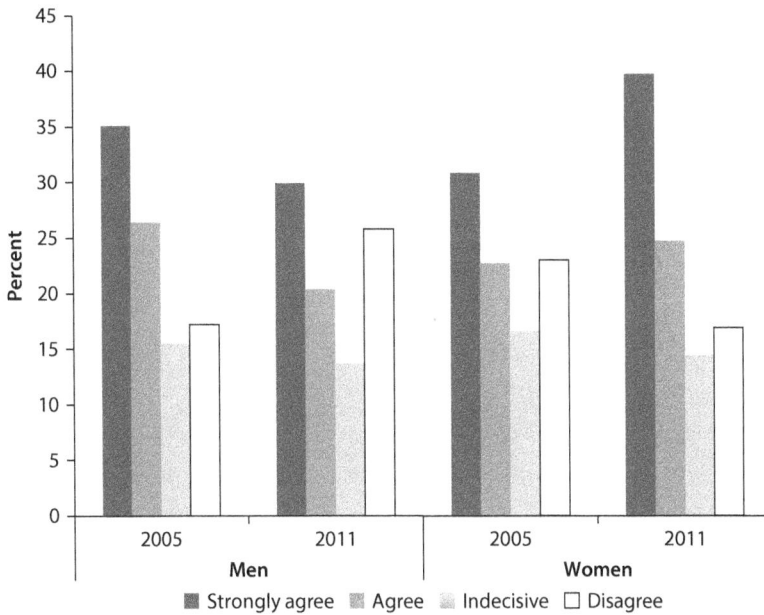

Source: Human Rights Commission of Maldives 2012.

should not be disclosed outside of the family. At the same time, and somewhat contradictory, both men and women are less likely to agree that a husband has to control his wife in all ways (table 3.1).

For yet other outcomes, men's and women's opinions appear to be diverging. For instance, between 2005 and 2011, the percentage of men who agreed or strongly agreed with the statement that "a man should never hit his wife" dropped significantly, whereas that of women increased (figure 3.14). Similarly, more women agreed—and more men disagreed—with statements asking whether a woman should be able to refuse sex with her husband if he is intoxicated or if she is sick (figure 3.15).

Decline in Support for Women's Rights in Other Aspects of the Private and Public Spheres

Support of women's rights in family matters and inheritance has also declined over time, in both urban and rural areas and across a range of spheres of life, from work to custody (Human Rights Commission of Maldives 2012). The only exception is a reported increase in support among urban respondents for women's rights to divorce, but unfortunately the report presenting these data did not provide any explanation (figures 3.16 and 3.17).

Erosion of Women's Political Participation

Women's political participation and support for such participation also seem to be eroding over the last few years. According to archival data from the

Figure 3.15 Change in Support for Women's Right to Refuse Marital Sex

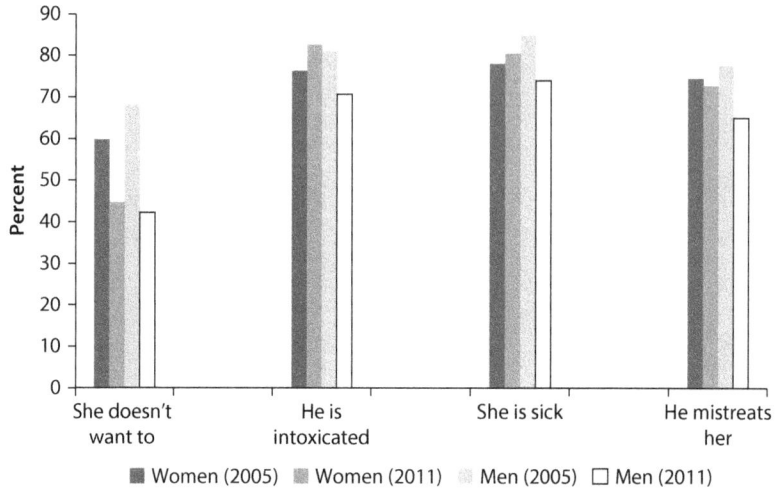

Source: Human Rights Commission of Maldives 2012.

Figure 3.16 Change in Support for Gender Equality: Rural Areas

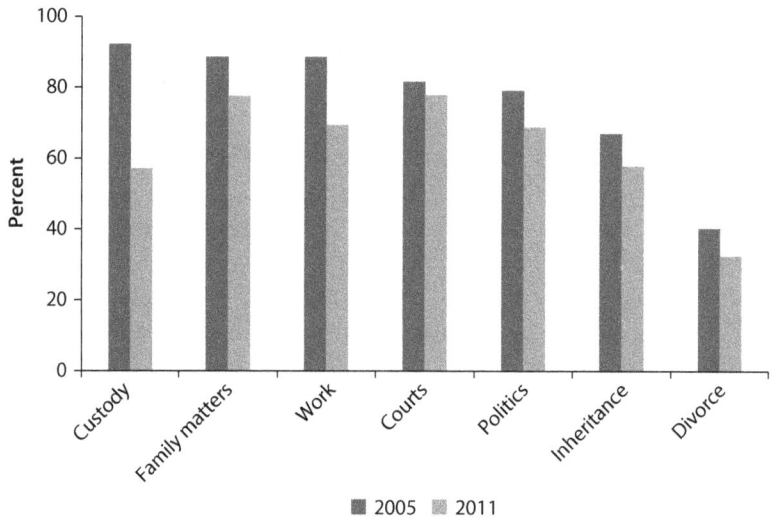

Source: Human Rights Commission of Maldives 2012.

Inter-Parliamentary Union (n.d.) women's political representation in the People's Majlis increased between 1989 and 2005 but has started to decline since then (figure 3.18).

Attitudes of men—but not of women—toward women's participation in politics and government match this trajectory. Between 2005 and 2011, the percent

Figure 3.17 Change in Support for Gender Equality: Urban Areas

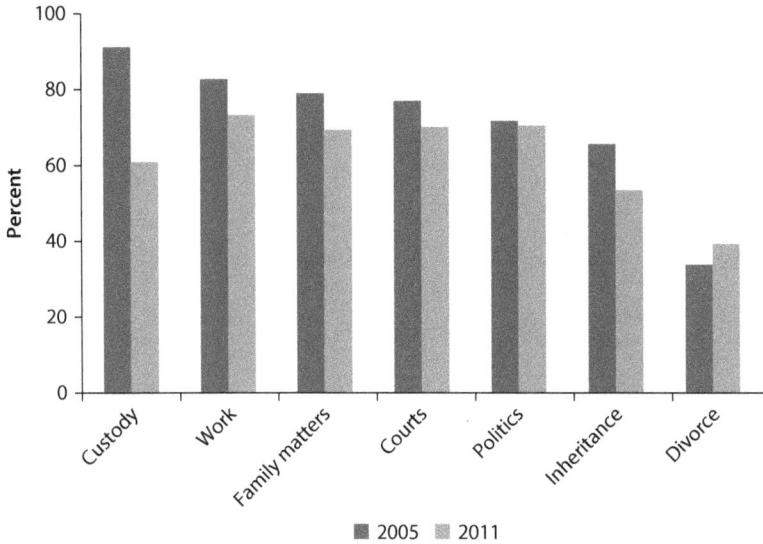

Source: Human Rights Commission of Maldives 2012.

Figure 3.18 Women's Representation in the People's Majlis

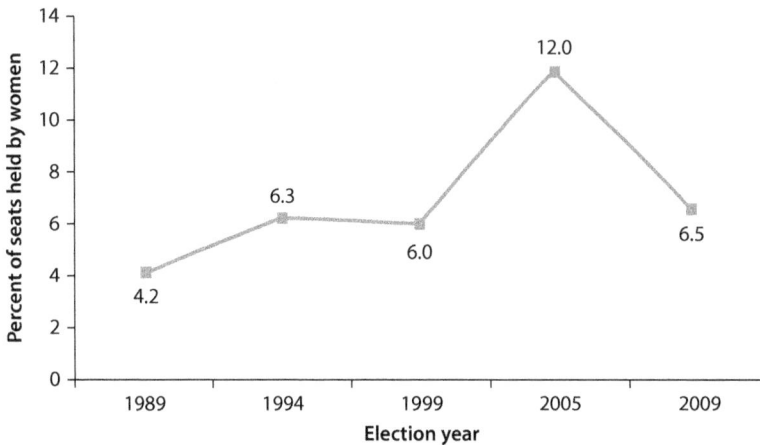

Source: Inter-Parliamentary Union, n.d.

of women supporting women's political participation stayed steady at around 80 percent, whereas the percent of men supporting women's political participation dropped notably from 72.9 percent to 57.6 percent (Human Rights Commission of Maldives 2012). These attitudes toward women's political participation likely cause the schism between the opportunities that are legally available to women for political participation and their actual experiences of

Figure 3.19 Support for Women's Rights in Maldives Tilting Away from Gender Equality

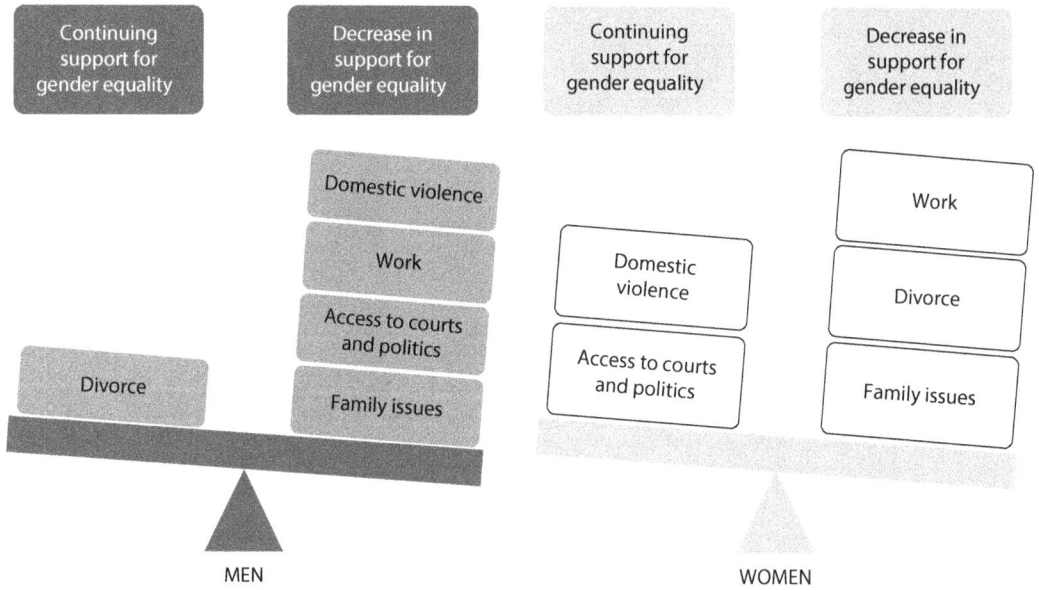

such participation. Although many countries in South Asia have responded to the lack of women in political leadership roles with reservations systems that instate quotas for women's political representation, Maldives has not yet taken such an action.

Overall, support for women's rights in different domains has tilted away from gender equality. Further, this is the case among men and women both (figure 3.19).

Notes

1. Based on 2014 data provided by the Ministry of Transport and Communications. Information referred to in ADB (2014).

2. Data for Malaysia are from Shuib et al. (2013). Other data are from the DHS for each country that was closest in year to Maldives 2009 DHS, with some of the data compiled by UN Women. http://www.endvawnow.org/uploads/browser/files/vaw _prevalence_matrix_15april_2011.pdf.

3. There are various sources of data on employment in Maldives, including data by the ILO, the World Bank, and the World Bank–Government of Maldives HIES 2009/10. Some include expatriates whereas others do not. Thus, figures are not strictly comparable and are provided here to illustrate ballpark ranges. We note in each case the source of data.

4. The labor force participation rate is defined as: "...the proportion of the population ages 15 and older that is economically active: all people who supply labor for the production of goods and services during a specified period" (World Development Indicators, http://data.worldbank.org/indicator/SL.TLF.CACT.ZS.).

5. The ILO definition of unemployment states that a person is unemployed if the person is 15 years and over; has no employment during the reference period; was

available for work, except for temporary illness; and had made specific efforts to find employment sometime during the reference week (Department of National Planning 2012, 41).

6. This definition of unemployment "…is much broader, and attempts to capture the local situation as there is hardly any job market in the islands and hence people usually do not regularly go seeking for work, with the belief that there are no jobs available in the island" (Department of National Planning 2012, 29).

7. The HIES 2009/10 defines "head of household" as either the husband (in a marital family), the sole occupant if living alone, and, in situations of a group of people, related or unrelated, co-residing, the person the respondent considers as the head or the eldest resident individual. Further details are on pages 103–4 of the HIES 2009/10 report (Department of National Planning 2012).

References

ADB (Asian Development Bank). 2014. *Maldives—Gender Equality Diagnostic of Selected Sectors*. Mandaluyong City, Philippines: Asian Development Bank.

Alder, C., and K. Polk. 2004. "Gender Issues in the Criminal Justice System of the Maldives." University of Melbourne, Department of Criminology, September 2. http://www.unicef.org/maldives/Gender_Issues_in_the_Criminal_Justice_System.pdf.

Asia Foundation and MIPSTAR (Maldives Institute for Psychological Services, Training and Research). 2012. *Rapid Situation Assessment of Gangs in Malé*. Colombo, Sri Lanka: The Asia Foundation.

Chitrakar, Roshan. 2009. *Overcoming Barriers to Girls' Education in South Asia: Deepening the Analysis*. Kathmandu, Nepal: United Nations Children's Fund Regional Office for South Asia (UNICEF ROSA).

Deere, Diana C., G. E. Alvarado, and J. Twyman. 2012. "Gender Inequality in Asset Ownership in Latin America: Female Owners vs. Household Heads." *Development and Change* 43 (2): 505–30.

Department of National Planning, Statistics Division, Republic of Maldives. 2012. *Household Income and Expenditure Survey 2009–2010*. Malé, Maldives: Government of Maldives.

Fulu, Emma. 2006. "Domestic Violence and Women's Health in Maldives." *Regional Health Forum* 11 (2): 25–32.

———. 2007a. *Maldives Study on Women's Health and Life Experiences: Initial Results on Prevalence, Health Outcomes and Women's Responses to Violence*. Malé, Maldives: Ministry of Gender and Family.

———. 2007b. "Gender, Vulnerability, and the Experts: Responding to the Maldives Tsunami." *Development and Change* 38 (5): 843–64.

———. 2014. *Domestic Violence in Asia: Globalization, Gender and Islam in Maldives*. London: Routledge.

Hope for Women. 2012. *Maldives NGO Shadow Report to the Committee on the Elimination of Discrimination against Women*. Malé, Maldives: Hope for Women.

Human Rights Commission of Maldives. 2012. *Six Years On—The Rights Side of Life*. The Second Maldives Baseline Human Rights Survey. Malé, Maldives: Human Rights Commission and UNDP (United Nations Development Programme).

ILO (International Labour Organization). 2013. *Global Employment Trends for Youth 2013: A Generation at Risk.* Geneva: ILO.

International Institute for Population Sciences (IIPS) and Macro International. 2007. *National Family Health Survey (NFHS-3), 2005–06: India.* Mumbai: IIPS.

International Trade Union Confederation. 2009. "Internationally Recognised Core Labour Standards in Maldives." Report for the World Trade Organization General Council Review of the Trade Policies of Maldives, Executive Summary, Geneva, October 26 and 28. http://www.ituccsi.org/IMG/pdf/Trade_Policy_Review_Maldives_final _october_09_.pdf.

Inter-Parliamentary Union. n.d. "Women in National Parliaments." http://www.ipu.org /wmn-e/classif.htm.

Ministry of Education, Republic of Maldives. n.d. *School Statistics 2014.* Malé, Maldives: Government of Maldives.

Ministry of Health and Gender, Republic of Maldives. 2014. *Maldives Health Profile—2014.* Malé, Maldives: Government of Maldives.

Ministry of Planning and National Development, Republic of Maldives. 2004. "Vulnerability and Poverty Assessment 2004." http://planning.gov.mv/Downloads /vpa/vpa2_book.pdf.

———. 2007. *Population and Housing Census 2006.* Malé, Maldives: Government of Maldives.

———. 2008. *Population and Housing Census 2006.* Analytical Report. Malé, Maldives: Government of Maldives. http://planning.gov.mv/en/images/stories/publications /analysiscd/#.

———. 2015a. *Population and Housing Census 2014.* Statistical Release III: Education. http://statisticsmaldives.gov.mv/nbs/wp-content/uploads/2016/02/StatisticalReleaseII -Education.pdf.

———. 2015b. *Population and Housing Census 2014.* Statistical Release IV: Employment. http://statisticsmaldives.gov.mv/nbs/wp-content/uploads/2016/02/StatisticalReleaseIV -Employment.pdf.

MOHF (Ministry of Health and Family, Republic of Maldives). 2007. *National Micronutrient Survey 2007.* Malé, Maldives: MOHF and United Nations Chidlren's Fund Maldives.

MOHF (Ministry of Health and Family, Republic of Maldives) and ICF Macro. 2010. *Maldives Demographic and Health Survey 2009.* Calverton, MD: MOHF and ICF Macro.

MOHP (Ministry of Health and Population, Nepal), New ERA, and ICF International Inc. 2012. *Nepal Demographic and Health Survey 2011.* Kathmandu, Nepal: MOHP; Calverton, MD: New ERA, and ICF International.

MPAO (Maldives Pension Administration Office). 2013. *Annual Report.* http://www .pension.gov.mv/uploads/downloads/annual-report/53ccdaa02dac4.pdf.

National Bureau of Statistics. 2016. *Statistical Yearbook of the Maldives 2015.* Government of Maldives. http://planning.gov.mv/yearbook2015/index.html#.

NIPORT (National Institute of Population Research and Training), Mitra and Associates, and Macro International. 2009. *Bangladesh Demographic and Health Survey 2007.* Calverton, MD: NIPORT, Mitra and Associates, and Macro International.

Ritchie, Megan, Terry Ann Rogers, and Lauren Sauer. 2014. *Women's Empowerment in Political Processes in Maldives.* Washington, DC: International Foundation for Electoral Systems.

Roul, Animesh. 2013. "The Threat from Rising Extremism in Maldives." *CTC Sentinel* 6 (3): 24–28. https://www.ctc.usma.edu/posts/the-threat-from-rising-extremism-in -the-maldives.

Shuib Rashidah, Noraida Endut, Siti Hawa Alib, Intan Osman, Sarimah Abdullah, Siti W. Oon, Puzziawati A. Ghani, Gaayathri Prabakaran, Nur S. Hussin, and Siti S.H. Shahrudin. 2013. "Domestic Violence and Women's Well-Being in Malaysia: Issues and Challenges Conducting a National Study using the WHO Multicountry Questionnaire on Women's Health and Domestic Violence against Women." *Procedia—Social and Behavioral Sciences* 91: 475–88.

Solotaroff, Jennifer L., and Rohini Prabha Pande. 2014. *Violence against Women and Girls: Lessons from South Asia.* South Asia Development Forum. Washington, DC: World Bank. https://openknowledge.worldbank.org/handle/10986/20153.

Swaminathan, H., R. Lahoti, and J. Y. Suchitra. 2012. "Women's Property, Mobility, and Decisionmaking: Evidence from Rural Karnataka, India." IFPRI Discussion Paper 1188, International Food Policy Research Institute. http://www.ifpri.org/sites/default/files /publications/ifpridp01188.pdf.

UNDP (United Nations Development Programme). 2011. *Women in Public Life in Maldives: A Situational Analysis.* Malé, Maldives: UNDP.

———. 2004. *Gender Issues in the Criminal Justice System of Maldives.* University of Melbourne, 2 September 2004.

UNFPA (United Nations Population Fund). 2005. *Maldives: Youth Voices Report 2005.* Malé, Maldives: UNFPA.

UNODC (United Nations Office on Drugs and Crime). 2013. *National Drug Use Survey. Maldives—2011/2012.* Malé, Maldives: UNODC.

UN Women (United Nations Entity for Gender Equality and the Empowerment of Women) and UNDP (United Nations Development Programme). 2014. *Maldivian Women's Vision Document.* Malé, Maldives: UNDP.

World Bank. 2012. *Enhancing the Quality of Education in Maldives: Challenges and Prospects.* South Asia Human Development Sector report no. 51. Washington, DC: World Bank.

———. 2014a. *World Development Indicators 2014.* Washington, DC: World Bank. http:// data.worldbank.org/indicator/SG.GEN.PARL.ZS.

———. 2014b. *Youth in Maldives: Shaping a New Future for Young Women and Men through Engagement and Empowerment.* Washington, DC: World Bank.

CHAPTER 4

Conclusion and Recommendations

Summary and Conclusions

In this report we have discussed gender differentials in various outcomes across the private and public spheres of life. We described how the dynamics between laws, custom and religion, and patterns of economic development influence these gender differentials. We also described how women's disadvantage in the private sphere of household relations could hamper their full participation in the public sphere, whether it is in education, employment, or political participation.

We find that gender differentials exist in some degree across all spheres of Maldivian life (figure 4.1). Gender inequality is least egregious in the most visible outcomes in the public sphere, such as education, health, and labor force participation, suggesting that gender egalitarian laws and policies in these spheres have been effective.

A clear female disadvantage persists, however, across outcomes in the private sphere, where increasing conservatism in social and cultural norms seems to take precedence over liberal laws and enhances ones that discriminate against women. Women face challenges that men do not, such as high risks of domestic violence, little control over household assets, and limited mobility. Women are underrepresented in politics and governance. Disaggregating national averages where data allow suggests that rural women and those in more remote atolls are likely to be particularly disadvantaged.

Time trends show a decline in societal support for women's voices and strong female roles in familial, social, economic, and political affairs, a shift that could further contribute to women's and girls' retreat from public social, political, and economic participation. Such a withdrawal, in turn, could weaken Maldives' accomplishments in gender equality to date and negatively affect future economic development.

Men face different gendered consequences of the current Maldivian economic, political, social, and religious landscape (figure 4.2). Qualitative and quantitative data suggest that notions of masculinity are changing from more gender egalitarian views to increasingly conservative preferences for the separation of gender roles inside and outside the home, with increasing primacy expected of men

Figure 4.1 Key Aspects of Female Disadvantage in Maldives

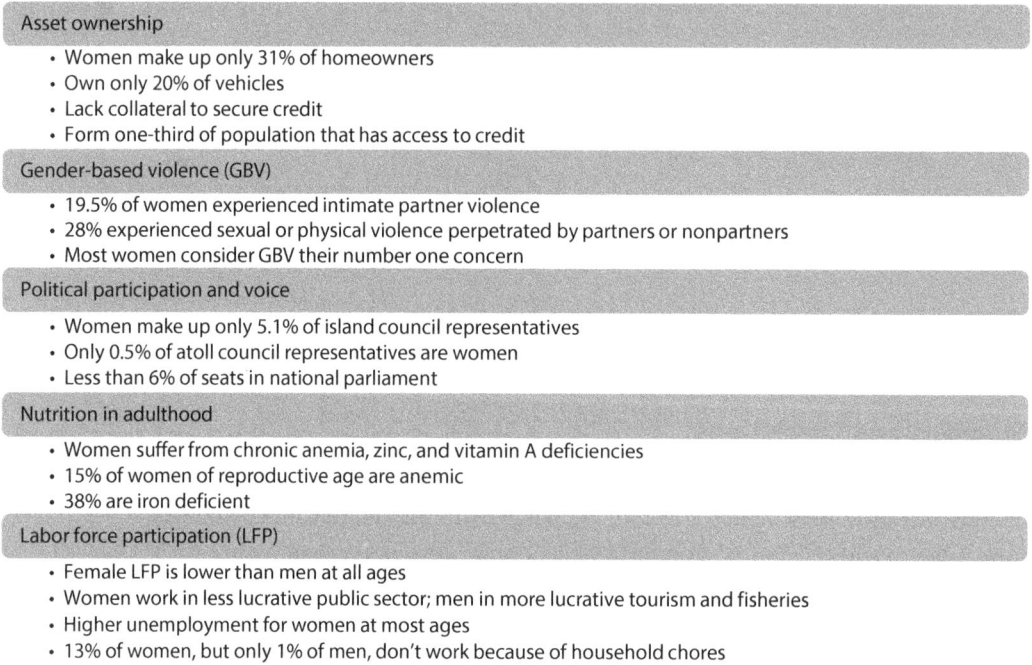

Asset ownership

- Women make up only 31% of homeowners
- Own only 20% of vehicles
- Lack collateral to secure credit
- Form one-third of population that has access to credit

Gender-based violence (GBV)

- 19.5% of women experienced intimate partner violence
- 28% experienced sexual or physical violence perpetrated by partners or nonpartners
- Most women consider GBV their number one concern

Political participation and voice

- Women make up only 5.1% of island council representatives
- Only 0.5% of atoll council representatives are women
- Less than 6% of seats in national parliament

Nutrition in adulthood

- Women suffer from chronic anemia, zinc, and vitamin A deficiencies
- 15% of women of reproductive age are anemic
- 38% are iron deficient

Labor force participation (LFP)

- Female LFP is lower than men at all ages
- Women work in less lucrative public sector; men in more lucrative tourism and fisheries
- Higher unemployment for women at most ages
- 13% of women, but only 1% of men, don't work because of household chores

Figure 4.2 Key Aspects of Male Disadvantage in Maldives

Gang participation	Substance abuse	Unemployment in youth	Educational attainment
• Mostly young men under the age of 25 years • Violent: interpersonal, political, and business-related violence • 2012: 20–30 gangs in Malé with 40–500 members in each	• 2014: 47% of Maldivian men smoke; 12% of women • 2013: 6% of male population abused drugs; mostly young men • 68% of youth identify drugs as major problem for young men	• Young men more likely to be unemployed than young women • Ages 15–19: 44% of men vs. 25% of women unemployed, 2010 • Ages 20–24: 23% of men vs. 20% of women unemployed, 2010 • Employability affected by gangs, lack of skills, and unrealistic aspirations	• Lower scores than girls in General Certificate Examination Ordinary and Advanced Levels

outside the home. At the same time, the dissatisfaction with current economic options outside of the home and the lack of an alternative structure to take the place of the breakdown of the traditional family structure are contributing to young men's growing participation in gangs, with concomitant implications for drug use and violence as they transition to full adulthood.

Our key informant interviews and an increasing body of research point to the shift in the nature of Islamic practice in Maldives as a key factor influencing gender inequality and roles for young women and young men, and one that increasingly contradicts the legal position of women. Many respondents noted that historically the daily practice of Islam has typically been relatively moderate: for instance, women's dress code and mobility in public spaces, as well as mingling between the sexes, have been less restricted than in many other Islamic countries. However, the recent expansion of a more conservative interpretation of Islam dictates a strict separation of roles and spaces for men and women, namely, confining the private sphere of the home and its responsibilities for women, and reserving access to the public sphere of society and its opportunities for men. The ubiquitous use of all means of media to publicize these messages has meant that Maldivians of all ages are exposed to this messaging.

Overall, gender inequality in Maldives appears to disadvantage women in more domains of life than is the case for men. In fact, Maldives exhibits a classic case of a relatively prosperous country where gender inequalities in basic well-being (in health and education) are largely diminished but where other social and cultural restrictions on women's abilities to make choices for their lives (in realms related to agency) persist and may be expanding. Furthermore, repeated surveys from 2005 and 2011 (Human Rights Commission of Maldives 2012) demonstrate that public support for gender equality and women's rights on various aspects of life, be it in the private sphere or the public sphere, appears to be declining. There is also a lessening of support for women's rights, including to work, coinciding with "…increasing exhortations by religious scholars for women to stay at home…" (Gunatilaka 2013; see also Department of National Planning 2008). For the most part, these changes in support are occurring in both urban and rural areas and—for a range of outcomes—among both women and men. These developments are worrying for the future of gender equality in Maldives, as well as for a more inclusive development model that would offer opportunities to both men and women, in youth and adulthood.

Recommendations

The analyses above illustrate that Maldives is at a crucial juncture in its development and highlight issues that require further attention by the Government of Maldives (GoM) and its development partners. Maldives has the distinction of being a middle-income country that has achieved or is close to achieving five of eight Millennium Development Goals. At the same time, there is tension in financial, economic, political, and social arenas, and a possible backslide on gender equality. Going forward, to build on the country's successes and avert reversals on social, gender, and political fronts, policy makers need to (1) strengthen social and governmental institutions in order to solidify existing gender equality gains, mitigate gender inequalities, and stem the current erosion of support for gender equality and (2) promote engagement with the large youth population—both young men and women—in innovative, equitable, inclusive ways in the country's economy and polity. Doing so requires strengthening and fully implementing the gender-egalitarian civil law of Maldives, building transparency and accountability to reduce mistrust and improve relations between the government and its citizens, and implementing policies and programming that target vulnerable youth of both genders who risk perpetuating social and economic instability. Influencing these types of change is a long-term process, which would require Maldives to adopt a broad strategy *toward a new social contract for greater transparency and egalitarian inclusion for both women and men.*

Below we present recommendations at the policy, data and research, and intervention levels pertinent to each of the key outcomes we consider. For each recommendation, we focus on the most critical level(s) at which we consider immediate action most important as per the report's findings. Table 4.1 provides a summary.

1. **Maintain a permanent ministry or department of gender, and increase the capacity of government staff to mainstream gender issues across sectors and ministries.** As evidenced, there exists a history of instability with regard to the government machinery tasked with ensuring gender equality; little continuity has existed between the bodies tasked with carrying forward a platform for equality. Additionally, there is limited capacity among government staff for effectively mainstreaming gender.

   Policy:
   - Promote a policy dialogue on gender issues that helps identify the most appropriate placement within the government for the gender ministry, and highlight capacities that need to be strengthened within this ministry and others to ensure mainstreaming.
   - Enact legislation to ensure a permanent location of the gender ministry, preventing any arbitrary shifting of the body.

   Research and Data:
   - Build capacity of staff of gender and sectoral ministries to collect, maintain, and analyze sex-disaggregated data on all outcomes of interest, including education, health, employment, and asset ownership.

2. **Bolster women's political participation at the local and national levels.** A body of evidence points to the fact that women are largely underrepresented in the political life of Maldives; at the local level there are few opportunities for women to participate in local government administration or as part of civil society, and at the national level political participation among women is even more limited. Among those women who do achieve high-ranking positions in government or within political parties, few represent the "average woman." A combination of cultural and religious barriers, as well as a lack of opportunity and knowledge on political matters, hinders their participation.

Table 4.1 Summary of Recommendations

Recommendation	Level of action		
	Policy	*Data and research*	*Interventions*
1. Ensure a permanent gender ministry or department	• Identify appropriate placement within government for gender ministry • Highlight capacity strengthening needs • Enact legislation to prevent arbitrary shifting of gender ministry/department	• Increase capacity to collect and analyze sex-disaggregated data across sectors	
2. Increase women's political participation	• Increase women's development committee budgets • Institute and implement quotas for women in national and local government		• Support women's civic and political training
3. Enhance women's mobility, property ownership, and access to credit		• Conduct more research to understand women's limited property rights and ownership • Collect data on women's mobility	• Implement initiatives to expand women's access to credit • Use media to raise awareness about parental and societal views inhibiting women's mobility • Encourage and facilitate women's ownership of means of transportation
4. Support youth inclusion	• Coordinate public messaging among ministries to promote youth engagement • Promote international peer-to-peer learning to address youth exclusion and unemployment	• Conduct survey of youth perceptions to better understand their perspective • Collect data on youth gangs, particularly outside of Malé	• Launch social innovation competitions to engage youth and increase the appeal of economic opportunities • Highlight positive youth role models via radio and film • Use media to engage with parents and address intergenerational gaps • Support government of Maldives in youth- and employer-driven job preparation
5. Improve public health programs		• Collect data and conduct analysis of adult gender differentials in nutritional status • Evaluate ongoing efforts to address drug abuse • Evaluate reasons for the government's limited capacity to provide reproductive health services	• Increase awareness of adult women's malnutrition • Learn from other countries how to successfully address malnutrition • Improve budgeting, training, and monitoring of de-addiction and rehabilitation centers • Link de-addiction centers with youth centers

table continues next page

Table 4.1 Summary of Recommendations *(continued)*

Recommendation	Policy	Data and research	Interventions
		Level of action	
6. Increase women's employment in high-growth sectors		• Conduct analysis to identify gaps in women's participation throughout the value chain in fisheries and tourism • Collect sex-disaggregated data to analyze gender wage gap • Highlight poverty implications of low-income status among female-headed households	• Encourage community efforts to address taboos for women's employment in key sectors • Increase backward-forward links to tourism among women-dominated industries • Build capacity of existing women's small and medium enterprises • Provide childcare at places of employment • Provide women's dormitories and other facilities that decrease familial reluctance to allow young women to travel for work
7. Mitigate women's vulnerability to gender-based violence (GBV)	• Ensure implementation and capacity building of current laws and drafted acts	• Collect data on trends, forms, perpetrators, disclosure, and access to care	• Train all care providers to screen for and recognize GBV and to provide services • Develop hotlines • Use media to increase awareness of GBV and its unacceptability

Policy:
- Increase budgets for women's development committees (WDCs) so that women leaders can have an increased opportunity to shape local development.
- Institute and implement quotas for women in national and local politics, learning from the successes and constraints faced by other regional experiences (for example, India's system of *panchayats*).

Interventions:
- Support women's civic training, for example by building on existing efforts by organizations such as the International Foundation for Electoral Systems (IFES).

3. **Target specific constraints that affect women's mobility, property ownership, and access to credit.** Although civil law is egalitarian, the analysis shows that social norms and interactions in the private sphere favor men's ownership of household assets and resources. A lack of access to property and other assets restricts women's access to credit, limits their mobility, and limits their exploration of entrepreneurial activities.

Understanding Gender in Maldives • http://dx.doi.org/10.1596/978-1-4648-0868-5

Research and Data:
• New research is needed to better understand the ownership (or lack thereof) of different types of property by women, as well as their rights to property.
• There is a dire need to collect additional data on women's mobility because existing quantitative data is very limited and out-of-date.

Interventions:
• Support women-targeted initiatives for expanding access to credit.
• Use media messages, role models, and success stories to raise awareness about parental and societal views on the acceptability of young women's traveling across islands alone, particularly for education or jobs.
• Encourage and facilitate women's access to and ownership of means of transportation (such as the motorcycles that are ubiquitous on the islands), through increasing access to easy or earmarked credit.

4. **Effectively and creatively engage with the youth to support their inclusion in a changing society.** The social, familial, economic, and political changes occur-ring rapidly and simultaneously in Maldives have contributed to the lack of urgency among young people to find employment and have left them searching for a new identity in a globalized world. Youth are growing increasingly discon-nected from family and society, and the result has been a high number of idle youth, that is, youth not in employment, education, or training (NEET). Young women find education and employment options limited. Young men may par-ticipate in gang activities because of a number of different motivating factors, and their problems are increasingly compounded by illicit drug use. Those who wish to reintegrate into society and participate in the labor market often face a dearth of support services. A range of actions may be required in policy, research and data, and intervention levels, some of which would address constraints faced by all youth, whereas others would focus specifically on the gendered con-straints identified in this report and faced by young men or young women.

Policy:
• Promote policy dialogue among key ministries (education, youth and sports, economic development) to initiate coordinated public messaging to promote youth engagement.
• Promote peer-to-peer learning (with other countries that have faced similar problems) on designing and implementing integrated initiatives to address youth exclusion, disenfranchisement, and unemployment.

Research and Data:
• Conduct a geographically and socially representative survey of youth's perceptions of, and grievances toward, society, including the government and private sector, to provide a broader understanding of why youth do not seize available employment and other opportunities.

- Collect more rigorous data pertaining to the number of gangs and members, reasons for youth to join gangs, and prevalence of gang violence, particularly outside of Malé, where little data exist.

Interventions:
- Launch a series of social innovation competitions among youth centers to promote active engagement and creativity of young people. Social innovation projects could be linked directly or indirectly to nearby resorts or tourism opportunities on the island and could include programs such as the rehabilitation of local cultural attractions for tourists, developing a youth-friendly platform for work opportunities in the resorts, and peer-to-peer mentoring for previous drug users. Globally, social innovations have been used as a tool to promote jobs as "cool" and desirable for young marginalized and idle youth (Kander 2013; Tucker 2014).
- Air a series of radio shows and videos to highlight positive role models of young Maldivians, and to engage with parents and address intergenerational gaps that have exacerbated youth unemployment and disenfranchisement.
- Establish a national public information campaign to counter stigma and taboos that negatively impact youth employment and public sphere engagement (especially for young women).
- Support the GoM in the design and implementation of targeted, youth- as well as employer-driven job preparation initiatives, providing them with both soft and hard skills to engage with the "new Maldivian economy."

5. **Support integrated public health programs to address key needs identified for women and for men.** While women and girls fare as well as or better than boys with regard to multiple indicators of basic health, deeper analysis reveals that women commonly suffer from malnutrition. On the other hand, young men are at higher risk of drug use, which has detrimental impacts on their employability, reintegration into society, and ability to access adequate rehabilitation services. Both young men and young women have no access to reproductive services, another lacuna in the health system.

Data and Research:
- Collect in-depth quantitative (measurement of anemia) and qualitative (food preferences and intake) sex- and age-disaggregated data on nutritional status that would enable a comprehensive analysis of why women are more malnourished than are men.
- Evaluate ongoing efforts to address drug abuse in order to identify approaches that have a potential for scale-up. Although there seem to be many active efforts, there has been little rigorous analysis of their success or lack thereof.
- Evaluate the reasons for the failure of the government health system to provide acceptable and effective reproductive health services to young women and men.

Interventions:
- Increase mass awareness of women's malnutrition as a problem, ensuring that society understands that it exists, why it exists, and why it is an important problem. Also educate citizens on what forms of malnutrition exist (such as anemia) and what families can do at home to address them (such as appropriate food intake, health care).
- Learn from other countries in South Asia or elsewhere that have developed successful approaches to address (particularly young) women's malnutrition. For instance, malnutrition among adolescent and young girls and women is a significant problem in India, and many programs exist to address this.
- Make de-addiction and rehabilitation centers functional: increase budgeting, train providers, increase public awareness about what these centers should provide, establish monitoring mechanisms, and consider linking these services with youth centers.

6. **Increase female employment in high-growth and high-employment sectors.** Women have been excluded from the burgeoning tourism industry, where several factors impede their participation. These factors include the social stigmas associated with young unmarried women staying on resort islands for significant periods of time, the perceived risk of women traveling alone, high costs of transport, and limited access to childcare facilities. Women have also been displaced from their traditional roles in Maldives' large fishing industry because of increasing mechanization. Tackling the low participation of women in these high-growth sectors could enable GoM to increase the country's overall female labor force participation and eventually close any gender wage gap.

Research and Data:
- Collect data and conduct analysis on women's participation through the value chain in fisheries and tourism, to assess where gaps exist.
- Collect sex-disaggregated data on hours worked, skills, tenure, and other variables that would enable rigorous analysis of the gender wage gap.
- Analyze and highlight particular poverty implications of low incomes among the female-headed households that this report identified.

Interventions:
- All interventions to support female employment in high-growth sectors should include a community mobilization activity that counters taboos and stigma attached to these sectors.
- Increase backward–forward links with industries that feed into tourism and that are women dominated, such as agriculture (which could provide food to the tourism sector).
- Provide services such as childcare that free up women (especially young women) to seek employment opportunities.
- Provide women's hostels and other facilities that make families less reluctant to allow women to travel for work. These hostels could also be used for

women and girl students, particularly to enable them to access tertiary education, similar to what has been accomplished through the Asian Development Bank's program on dormitories (ADB 2014).

7. **Mitigate women's vulnerability to gender-based violence (GBV).** As described, over one-quarter of Maldivian women have experienced physical or sexual violence at some point in their lives. Such violence is perpetrated in both public and private spaces and has been identified as a major concern by women. GBV has deleterious effects not only on women's health but also on the overall development process in Maldives.

Research and Data:
- Address the serious lack of data on (1) trends since the Demographic and Health Survey of 2009; (2) forms of violence other than intimate partner violence, such as violence on the streets, violence in the workplace, and so on; (3) perpetrators; (4) disclosure; and (5) access to care.

Interventions:
- Sensitize and train all care providers to screen for and recognize GBV and to provide needed services to survivors of violence. Police, the judiciary, and health care service providers are key individuals to be sensitized and trained. Build on the documented evaluations of such programs worldwide on what works and what doesn't for effective training.
- Develop hotlines, learning from other country experiences on successful and unsuccessful endeavors.
- Use media to spread a message of the unacceptability of violence against women and girls, whether in the home or outside of the home. Examples to build on from across the world include "real men don't beat their wives and daughters" and "equality as citizens," among others.

A Final Word on Approaches for Programming

Maldives has a range of gender-egalitarian policies as well as youth programming that reaches young men and young women alike. However, there is almost no information on their implementation or effectiveness. For instance, in research conducted for this report and the World Bank's earlier youth report (World Bank 2014), several interviewees described a process whereby new programs—for youth or to address gender concerns—would start and end within the span of a year or two without any analysis of factors that led to the closure of the program and with no information about the impact of the program, including limitations and challenges faced. To break this pattern, any new initiatives would need to be structured so as to be part of national planning. Initiatives would also need to be designed with enough funds, time, and ability to get the desired expertise to collect sex-disaggregated data and conduct appropriate impact evaluations to inform future interventions and strategies. Such initiatives are certainly costly, but in the long term they can save money by ensuring that resources intended to improve gender equality are allocated to well-designed, well-implemented programs with a high probability of success.

Finally, Maldives needs to continue to cement gains in gender equality achieved thus far, and lessen discriminatory gender differentials where they exist, particularly for the youth that comprise the majority of the population. Gender-discriminatory, patriarchal attitudes and norms, emphasized by increasingly conservative streams of Islam, can hold back both men and women, especially in adolescence and young adulthood, and can threaten the country's political stability, social cohesion, and economic development. Any policy making or programming in Maldives needs to be sensitized to counter the appeal of radicalism and to further expand the country's horizons in the domains of education, employment, health and survival, and economic development itself.

References

ADB (Asian Development Bank). 2014. *Maldives—Gender Equality Diagnostic of Selected Sectors*. Mandaluyong City, Philippines: ADB.

Department of National Planning, Republic of Maldives. 2008. *Increasing Female Labour Force Participation in Maldives*. Malé, Maldives: Government of Maldives.

Gunatilaka, Ramani. 2013. *Employment Challenges in Maldives*. Geneva: International Labour Organization.

Human Rights Commission of Maldives. 2012. *Six Years On—The Rights Side of Life*. The Second Maldives Baseline Human Rights Survey. Malé, Maldives: Human Rights Commission and UNDP (United Nations Development Programme).

Kander, Rosabeth Moss. 2013. "Jobs and Social Innovation." *Stanford Social Innovation Review* (Spring). http://www.hbs.edu/faculty/Publication%20Files/Spring_2013_Jobs _and_Social_Innovation_feb41812-f3da-4025-9a4d-856d558e7e9c.pdf.

Tucker, Simon. 2014. *Social Innovation for Public Service Excellence*. Singapore: UNDP Global Centre for Public Service Excellence. http://www.undp.org/content/dam/uspc /docs/GPCSE_Social%20Innovation.pdf.

World Bank. 2014. *Youth in Maldives: Shaping a New Future for Young Women and Men through Engagement and Empowerment*. Washington, DC: World Bank.

Environmental Benefits Statement

The World Bank Group is committed to reducing its environmental footprint. In support of this commitment, the Publishing and Knowledge Division leverages electronic publishing options and print-on-demand technology, which is located in regional hubs worldwide. Together, these initiatives enable print runs to be lowered and shipping distances decreased, resulting in reduced paper consumption, chemical use, greenhouse gas emissions, and waste.

The Publishing and Knowledge Division follows the recommended standards for paper use set by the Green Press Initiative. The majority of our books are printed on Forest Stewardship Council (FSC)–certified paper, with nearly all containing 50–100 percent recycled content. The recycled fiber in our book paper is either unbleached or bleached using totally chlorine-free (TCF), processed chlorine-free (PCF), or enhanced elemental chlorine-free (EECF) processes.

More information about the Bank's environmental philosophy can be found at http://www.worldbank.org/corporateresponsibility.

green press INITIATIVE

www.ingramcontent.com/pod-product-compliance
Lightning Source LLC
Chambersburg PA
CBHW080002280326

41935CB00013B/1730